STUART PATERSON

Stuart Paterson's children's plays, first performed at Glasgow's Citizen's Theatre, Edinburgh's Royal Lyceum, Dundee Repertory Theatre and Newcastle Playhouse, have since been staged throughout the UK. They include *Merlin The Magnificent*, *The Snow Queen*, *Beauty and the Beast*, *Cinderella*, *Granny and the Gorilla*, *The Princess and the Goblin*, *The Sleeping Beauty*, a one-act play *The Secret Voice*, and an adaptation of Roald Dahl's *George's Marvellous Medicine*. In 1998 *Hansel and Gretel* was nominated for the Barclays Best Children's Production of the Year Award.

He has written *King of the Fields* for the Traverse Theatre and new versions of Chekhov's *The Cherry Orchard* and *Uncle Vanya*. For The Scottish Youth Theatre he has written *In Traction* (later televised by BBC) and adapted Zola's *Germinal*. He has also adapted Zola's *Therese Raquin* for Communicado Theatre Company, which was also staged at Newcastle Playhouse and Edinburgh's Royal Lyceum. His work for Tag Theatre Company includes an adaptation of James Hogg's *The Private Memoirs and Confessions of a Justified Sinner*, and a new version of J. M. Barrie's *Peter Pan* staged at the Royal Lyceum, Edinburgh. He has recently completed a new version of *Comrades* by August Strindberg for the Royal Lyceum and an adaptation of *The Ballroom of Romance* by William Trevor for Northern Stage.

His television credits include *The Old Course* (BBC) and the film *Workhorses*, which won The Pharic Mclaren Award.

His short film *Somebody's Wee Nobody* won the Gold Award at the Chicago International Film Festival. Current film projects include original screenplays *The Pretender*, *Whisky Mac*, *Under the Same Moon*, *The Chieftain's Daughter* and screen adaptations of *The Kelpie's Pearls* by Mollie Hunter, *Fergus Lanont* by Robin Jenkins and Shusaku Edo's *Scandal*.

Other Titles in this Series

STUART PATERSON

Hansel and Gretel

with an Afterword by the author
and music by Savourna Stevenson

NICK HERN BOOKS
London
www.nickhernbooks.co.uk

A Nick Hern Book

Hansel and Gretel first published in Great Britain in 2000
as an original paperback by Nick Hern Books Limited,
14 Larden Road, London W3 7ST

Hansel and Gretel © 2000 by Stuart Paterson

Music © 2000 by Savourna Stevenson

Stuart Paterson has asserted his right to be identified
as the author of this work

Front cover illustration copyright © Sophie Herxheimer

Typeset by Country Setting, Kingsdown, Kent CT14 8ES

Printed and bound in Great Britain by Biddles, Guildford

A CIP catalogue record for this book is available from
the British Library

ISBN 1-85459 483-4

To Joan, Alana, Patrick and Bruno
with love and thanks

Hansel and Gretal was first performed at the Royal Lyceum Theatre, Edinburgh, on 2 December 1998, with the following cast:

ORIN	Michael Mackenzie
CONAL/MONKEY	Malcolm Shields
BANSHEE / STEPMOTHER/	
LA STREGAMAMA	Irene MacDougall
HANSEL	Billy Boyd
GRETEL	Caroline Devlin
FATHER/ LOB	Eric Barlow
RAB	Antony Somers
MOFF	Philippa Vafadari
UNCLE SHOES	Alan Steele

Director Hugh Hodgart
Designer Gregory Smith
Composer Savourna Stevenson
Choreographer Malcolm Shields
Lighting Designer Davy Cunningham
Musical Director Jon Beales

'If I Were a King ... ' and 'If I Were a Queen ... ' on pages 45, 51, and 82 by Christina Rossetti.

'Do You Ask What the Birds Say? ....' on page 46 taken from 'Answer to a Child's Question' by Samuel Taylor Coleridge.

Lyrics to 'La Stregamama' on pages 53 and 54 by Nicholas Gibbon and Stuart Paterson.

Characters

HANSEL
GRETEL
FATHER
STEPMOTHER
ORIN
CONAL
BANSHEE / LA STREGAMAMA
YOUNG GIRL
RAB
MOFF
LOB
MONKEY

Possible doubling for a cast of nine:

CONAL / MONKEY
BANSHEE / STEPMOTHER / LA STREGAMAMA
FATHER / LOB

Other doublings are possible.

ACT ONE

Scene One

Night-time. The mouth of a cave deep in the heart of The Wild Forest. Distant volcanic rumblings from within. Flames spark and flash like lightning amidst the drifting smoke. A witch's voice carries on the smoke.

VOICE.
Hey-How for Halloween!
Time to wake, oh Witch's Queen,
Time for me to be up and seen.
Hey-How for Halloween!

Enter ORIN, *The Faerie-King, and his son* CONAL.

ORIN. Behold The Cave of Fires, where the great witch Banshee lies imprisoned by The World's Magic.

CONAL (*amazed and delighted*). The Cave of Fires . . . I have heard it goes down and down to the flames that burn at the very heart of the world . . . Rock and stone melt in that oven like ice . . . (*Goes too close.*)

ORIN. Stay back! Daft boy, listen to what I tell you!

CONAL (*a little resentful*). I'm listening, Father, you don't have to shout.

ORIN. This is a magic place, and soon Halloween will come and The Witching Hour will be her doorway to the world. When midnight strikes she will try to break free from her fiery prison, and so wake all witches to their wicked work. (*Stands in front of the cave, raises his staff.*) She is the cruellest witch of all and must not go free! My magic will stop her!

CONAL. Let me stop her.

ORIN. I am Faerie-King, and it is my duty.

CONAL. And I am your son, and must help my father in his
work.

ORIN. Another year, when you are grown . . .

CONAL. How can I grow when you won't let me? I know
enough of magic . . . You've taught me to dive with fishes,
to soar with the birds into the wind and out again . . .

ORIN. There is more to this magic than tricks and games.

CONAL. Then give me work, father, so that I may learn.

ORIN. You're not ready.

CONAL. I'm ready, father.

ORIN. She's the Queen Of Witches, and mother of all
mischief.

CONAL. I am ready.

ORIN. Here then, boy, take my staff . . .

CONAL. Thank you, father . . .

ORIN. Don't thank me! You must stand guard till dawn! Stand
straight, hold up the staff, plant it firm in the ground so it
has roots in your endeavour . . . That's the way. The staff
has great power. If it bars her way she cannot pass by.
Remember!

CONAL. Yes, father.

ORIN. When she comes, and come she must, do not speak
with her for she may trick you with clever words. Believe
nothing. Say nothing. Think nothing but your own thoughts.
Remember!

CONAL. I won't forget.

ORIN. Then you will do me honour, and in the morning I will
greet you as a man and my equal.

CONAL. Until the morning, father.

ORIN. Brave boy. Until the morning. (*Exits.*)

CONAL *holds his position for a few moments, then begins
to fidget.*

CONAL. The Staff Of The World's Magic! (*Brandishes it in a heroic fashion.*)

Rowan, lammer and red seed
Puts witches to their speed!

(*Throws the staff, catches it, fights and defeats imaginary witches and goblins.*) My father is such a fool . . . What harm can come to me? (*Slays another demon.*) I am a Prince of Magic . . . (*To the heavens.*) Come fight me, you dark spirits of the night, I challenge you all! Come out you hags and giants, come forth you witches, firedrakes and demons! I am afraid of nothing! (*A distant bell begins to toll causing him to start with fright.*) What sounds there? (*Relaxes.*) Nothing but the tower bell . . . But it sounds midnight and that's . . . that's The Witching Hour. (*Stands guard.*) Come on then, witch! I'm ready for you, in all your power and fury! (*A quiet sobbing comes from the cave.*) What's this? Tears?

VOICE (*a young girl's voice, through sobs*). Help me . . . Someone help me . . . Please . . .

CONAL. Such a sweet voice . . .

VOICE. Oh the flames, the burning flames . . . Help me . . . Set me free . . .

CONAL. Put away these tricks . . . Show yourself, witch!

A beautiful YOUNG GIRL *appears from the smoke.*

YOUNG GIRL. Oh the flames, the burning flames . . . Help me . . .

CONAL. More like an angel than a witch . . . I must not believe my eyes . . . Get back from me! (*Holds staff firm.*) You shall not pass!

YOUNG GIRL (*sinking to her knees*). The pain . . . I will catch fire . . . Please . . . (*Sobs.*)

CONAL. No creature should suffer such pain . . . Her eyes . . . Her soft hair . . .

YOUNG GIRL (*reaching out her arms*). Please . . . Help me . . .

CONAL. And what if the witch does come? I'll pick her up and throw her back into the fire . . . Come, girl, come quickly. (*Lays down staff.*) I have laid down my guard . . .

The YOUNG GIRL *throws back her head and screams in triumph. A mighty explosion and* BANSHEE *appears in her true and terrifying form.*

BANSHEE. Haaaa! I have tricked you! Banshee is free! (CONAL *picks up the staff, but* BANSHEE *gestures and the staff flies to her hand.*) Foolish boy, the power is mine now! The power is mine!

CONAL (*running away*). Father, help me . . .

BANSHEE. Be still, boy! (*Gestures and* CONAL *is caught in her spell.*)

CONAL. I can't move!

BANSHEE. Why run away? Don't you think I'm pretty any more?

Enter ORIN.

ORIN. Leave him be, witch!

CONAL (*running to him*). Forgive me, father . . .

BANSHEE. Be still! (*She gestures and he is caught again in her spell.*)

ORIN. Set him free!

BANSHEE. Never! He will come with me, won't you, my little pet? (*Gestures, and* CONAL *is drawn slowly towards her.*)

CONAL. I can't help myself . . .

ORIN. Let him go! I command it!

BANSHEE. Old fool! You are king of nothing! (*Brandishes Orin's staff aloft.*) Bow to the new Queen! Bow down your head! (ORIN *is forced to his knees.*) I have your staff, I have my freedom, and now I will take your son.

ORIN. No!

BANSHEE. How lonely you will be without him. Come, my pet. (*Strokes* CONAL*'s face.*) You are mine now, forever.

CONAL. Father . . .

BANSHEE.
By all that will bite and scratch and tear,
Take him far from his father's care!

I command it! (*A bright flash and he vanishes.*)

ORIN. My son . . . Where is he?

BANSHEE. Where you will never find him, or me. Foolish man, to match a boy against a witch. I leave you now. Let misery be your prison! Away, I command it! (*A bright flash, and she vanishes.*)

ORIN. To lose my son . . . My heart is broken and the world is dead . . . But to lose hope is to make The Witch strong . . . I'll find him witch! I'll search this forest, and I'll find him! By all The World's Magic, I have sworn it!

Scene Two

A woodcutter's house, poor and simply furnished. HANSEL *looks out a window, keeping guard.* GRETEL, *holding a knife, tiptoes towards a table where there is a loaf and cheese, and a jug of milk.*

GRETEL. Is she coming?

HANSEL. No . . . Go on . . .

GRETEL (*losing her nerve*). I can't do it. She'll catch us.

HANSEL. I'll do it, then.

GRETEL. No, I will! Keep looking!

HANSEL. I am looking!

GRETEL. I hate our new mother . . . She creeps about as quiet as a snake.

HANSEL. Hurry up, I'm starving!

GRETEL. Sometimes I think she's a witch . . . (*Prepares to cut bread.*) Maybe if I cut the thinnest slice she won't notice . . .

HANSEL. She's coming! (GRETEL *nearly jumps out of her skin, hurries to* HANSEL's *side.*) There's no-one, Gretel, I'm sorry . . .

GRETEL. Don't do that!

HANSEL. I didn't do it on purpose!

GRETEL. I know you didn't . . . She scares me too.

HANSEL. I wish she would beat us with a stick then we could show father the wounds and he would send her away.

GRETEL. Instead she beats us with her smiles and her sweet voice . . .

HANSEL. And all the time she hates us even more than we hate her.

GRETEL. If only our real mother were still alive . . .

HANSEL. Don't cry, sister . . . What good are tears? They just make your face wet. I'll look after you . . . (*He takes the knife from her, approaches the table.*) Why shouldn't we eat? We're hungry, aren't we?

GRETEL. Be careful.

HANSEL. I won't be scared any more . . . . Do you ever dream, Gretel, dream that we're not poor, and have everything we want? (*Cuts a thin slice of bread.*) Come over here . . . Come on . . . (GRETEL *leaves the window, goes over to him.*) This is not stale bread, it's honey cake covered in sugar and wild berries . . . Open wide. (*He puts the bread into her mouth.*)

GRETEL (*her eyes closed*). Oh yes, wonderful . . . And this isn't old cheese, it's a sugar-loaf all wrapped in the thickest chocolate . . . Taste it . . . (*Puts cheese into his mouth.*)

HANSEL. Delicious . . . And this isn't goat's milk, it's juice from the ripest strawberries mixed with cream . . . Drink. (*She drinks from the jug.*)

GRETEL. Heaven . . . You try. (*He drinks from the jug.*)

HANSEL. Heaven . . .

The door opens and their STEPMOTHER *comes in.*

STEPMOTHER (*with icy sweetness*). Good evening, my dears.

HANSEL *and* GRETEL *have jumped with fright.*

GRETEL. It's you . . . I mean, we didn't see you . . .

STEPMOTHER. Ah yes, but I see you, I see what you've been up to . . . Stealing food from your father's table!

HANSEL. It's not stealing!

STEPMOTHER. What is it, then? Tell me that.

HANSEL. We only took a little.

STEPMOTHER. If I hadn't come in when I did you'd have gobbled up the lot and left your father and I nothing but crumbs . . . Gobble, gobble, gobble . . . Greedy little brats!

GRETEL. That's not true!

STEPMOTHER. I'll decide what's true! You're thieves, you've been caught, and now you must be punished! I'm afraid I'll have to tell your father.

HANSEL. Do what you like.

STEPMOTHER (*with a sweet smile*). Not that it gives me any pleasure. It's entirely for your own good.

Enter FATHER, *a gruff and kindly man worn by hard work and poverty.* HANSEL *and* GRETEL *run and embrace him.*

FATHER (*returning their embrace*). I see you, you little monkeys, I see you.

STEPMOTHER. Sad news, husband. All the time we've been cutting wood in the forest, Hansel and Gretel have been lying on their backs stealing the food from out of our mouths.

FATHER. Stealing food! Is this true? (HANSEL *and* GRETEL *can't look at him.*) Answer me! Is this true?

HANSEL *and* GRETEL (*in unison*). Yes, father.

FATHER. You know there's hardly enough to go around! We sit down together at table and share our food! Is that understood?

HANSEL *and* GRETEL (*in unison*). Yes, father.

STEPMOTHER (*quietly triumphant*). They must be sent to bed without any supper.

FATHER (*looking at the food on the table*). They didn't take much.

STEPMOTHER. Oh, but they must be punished.

FATHER (*working up a rage at the world*). They've been told, and that's the finish of it!

HANSEL *and* GRETEL *make faces at the* STEPMOTHER *from behind their* FATHER*'s back.*

STEPMOTHER (*to* HANSEL *and* GRETEL). Don't think you'll get away with this!

FATHER. Finish, I say!

STEPMOTHER (*with a meek smile*). Of course, dear husband.

FATHER. Five minutes peace . . . Is that too much to ask? So tired my bones hurt . . .

GRETEL. Sit in your chair, father. (*He sits down.*)

FATHER. Just need to put my head down . . . Five minutes . . . (HANSEL *pulls up a stool for his feet.*) Five minutes, and then we'll eat . . . (*Pulls hat down over his eyes, sleeps.*)

STEPMOTHER *angrily sets the table.*

GRETEL (*her eyes sparkling with mischief*). Is there anything we can do to help?

STEPMOTHER. Don't give me your cheek!

HANSEL. Sssh, quiet, you'll wake father.

STEPMOTHER (*boiling angry, and yet forced to speak in a half-whisper*). Oh, I'm warning you! You'll drive me mad, the pair of you!

GRETEL. We don't drive you mad.

HANSEL. You do that all by yourself.

STEPMOTHER (*stammering with rage*). I . . . I . . . I come into this family, I do all in my power to help you, and what do I get for my trouble? Insolence, nothing but the purest insolence . . .

GRETEL. We don't want your help!

STEPMOTHER. Horrible children . . . You've made my head hurt . . . (*Weeps.*)

HANSEL. And don't pretend to cry . . . It might work with father, but it doesn't work with us.

STEPMOTHER (*recovers instantly*). You know what you are don't you? You're spoiled, lazy, dirty little brats! And being poor is no excuse . . . I'm poor too, but that doesn't stop me making the best of myself, looking my best, doing my best . . . You should try to grow up to be like me.

GRETEL. Never . . .

HANSEL. Ever . . .

GRETEL. Ever!

STEPMOTHER. You know what I'm going to do to you, don't you? (FATHER *snores lightly.*)

HANSEL. What?

STEPMOTHER (*rubbing her head*). What?

GRETEL. What are you going to do to us?

STEPMOTHER. Oh yes . . . I'm going to teach you a lesson you'll never forget! And you won't be able to stop me. Do you know why? Mmm, do you?

HANSEL *and* GRETEL (*in unison*). No.

STEPMOTHER. You won't be able to stop me because I'm older than you, I'm bigger than you, I'm better than you, and I'm far, far cleverer than you! Oh yes, I'm going to teach you a lesson, don't you worry your pretty little heads.

(*Smiles brightly.*) On with my work, then . . . On, on, on . . . (*Returns to her work, humming with a creepy cheerfulness.*)

HANSEL *and* GRETEL *laugh with pent-up nerves and fear.*

GRETEL. It's not funny, Hansel . . .

HANSEL. I know . . . We've got to get her before she gets us.

GRETEL. We've absolutely got to!

HANSEL. But do you really think she is a witch?

GRETEL. How else could she be so horrible?

HANSEL. But how can we make father believe us?

GRETEL. I wonder . . . (*Goes over to where some of her father's work is stored.*) Look, Hansel . . . (*Picks up a broomstick.*) Look at the new broomstick father has made.

HANSEL. So?

GRETEL. Think, stupid.

HANSEL. Of course! Witches fly broomsticks!

GRETEL. And?

HANSEL. If we try it on her we'll find out if she really is a witch.

GRETEL. No witch could resist a broomstick as beautiful as this. (*Sits astride the broom.*)

HANSEL. Go on, see what happens. Maybe she'll fly away and leave us.

GRETEL. Oh, yes!

HANSEL. Or maybe she'll turn us into snakes.

GRETEL. You do it.

HANSEL. Alright, then.

GRETEL. No, it was my idea . . . Here I go . . . (*She moves closer to her* STEPMOTHER, *makes a show of sweeping the floor. Her* STEPMOTHER *takes a dizzy turn, her head moving in time with* GRETEL*'s broom.*) Is something the matter?

STEPMOTHER. Something's wrong . . . With my head . . . Get out of my way, girl! Can't you see I'm busy?

GRETEL. I'm just trying to help.

STEPMOTHER. When have you ever been any help? Like all children, you're a useless, lazy little worm. (*Sees the broomstick, comes alive with excitement.*) What's that?

GRETEL. What's what, stepmother?

STEPMOTHER. That there! In your hand!

GRETEL. This? Oh, it's only a new broomstick father has made.

STEPMOTHER. A new one?

GRETEL. Brand new.

STEPMOTHER. Give it to me!

GRETEL. But I'm working.

STEPMOTHER. Give it to me! I must have it! Now! This minute! Or I'll pull all the hair out of your head one hair at a time and stick your head in a beehive! Give it to me! Nooooowwwww! (GRETEL *gives it to her and runs to* HANSEL. *They watch with mischief and wonder.*) Oh wonderful stick, oh most beautiful broom . . . (*Holds it against her cheek.*) What craft is here . . . (S*niffs at the wood.*) It even smells of the moon and the forest at night after it has rained . . . (*Shivers with joy.*) Oh, to fly . . . (*Bestrides the broomstick, clutching it for dear life.*) To fly above the world! To fly higher and faster than the mightiest eagle with my hair flowing behind me like a comet's tail! And never to be poor! Never to have to scrimp or save, or bake or clean or stitch or sew! Demons will stitch my gowns, elves and firedrakes forge my golden shoes! Goblins will cook for me, hags brew my wine! And never to have to smile sweet smiles when you long to bite and scratch and tear! And never to have to pretend to be happy when you're fed up to the back teeth! Oh, the joy, the joy! (*Turns on* HANSEL *and* GRETEL.) And never, oh best of all, never to have to be kind to children, especially to vile little brats that

don't even belong to me! Oh, the things I could do!
(*Advances slowly on them, smiling sweetly.*) I could lock
you up in a tree, I could give you hooves instead of feet!
I could cook you up for tea . . . Oh, what a treat! I'll get you
alright, I'll get you . . . (HANSEL *and* GRETEL *back away
from her.*) But what's the matter, my dears? You're not
afraid of your new mother, are you? (*Laughs evilly.*) You're
not afraid of your sweet little stepmother?

GRETEL (*terrified, still backing away*). No, no, we like you . . .

HANSEL (*terrified, still backing away*). We've always liked
you . . . You're the best.

STEPMOTHER. Then, come closer, my dears.

GRETEL. We'd like to . . . Honest we would . . .

STEPMOTHER. Come closer, so I can get my hands on you.

GRETEL (*finally reaches her* FATHER). Father, wake up!
(*Shakes him.*)

STEPMOTHER. To fly, to fly!

HANSEL. Wake up, father, please!

FATHER. What's going on!

GRETEL. She's a witch, father!

HANSEL. You've got to believe us now. Look at her.

FATHER *looks at his new wife, but she is calmly sweeping
the floor.*

STEPMOTHER. Oh, my poor dear, have the children woken
you?

HANSEL. She's a witch, she really is!

FATHER. Mind your manners, girl!

GRETEL (*indicates* AUDIENCE). They'll tell you! (*To*
AUDIENCE.) She's a witch, isn't she?

AUDIENCE. Yes!

STEPMOTHER. Such cruelty . . . (*Tearfully.*) They'll break my
heart . . .

GRETEL. She's putting it on . . .

HANSEL. It's all just a stupid act. (*To* AUDIENCE.) She really is a witch, isn't she?

AUDIENCE. Yes!

FATHER. Stop all your nonsense!

GRETEL. Father, why won't you listen?

STEPMOTHER. Because he's a clever grown-up man and you're nothing but cheeky, ungrateful, lying little babies!

FATHER (*like thunder*). Be quiet, the lot of you!

STEPMOTHER (*tearfully*). Do you see what I have to put up with? And I love them so much.

FATHER (*putting his arm around her*). I know you do.

GRETEL. She doesn't love us!

HANSEL. She hates us!

GRETEL. And we hate her!

FATHER. I won't listen to this! Get out of my sight, the pair of you! Straight to bed!

STEPMOTHER. And no supper . . . Go on, you heard your father.

HANSEL. You wanted this . . . You love this . . .

FATHER. To bed! Now!

GRETEL. Come on, Hansel, leave them . . . (*They go to bed, in plain view, cuddling up together under their blanket.*)

STEPMOTHER. I'm sorry . . . I do all in my power . . .

FATHER. Don't blame yourself . . . (*Kisses her forehead.*) They still miss their mother . . .

STEPMOTHER. Come and eat . . . There's plenty for us . . .

FATHER. You eat . . . (*Tears off a hunk of bread.*) I have to speak to them.

STEPMOTHER. Of course you do . . .

FATHER. I can't leave it like this . . . (*Goes over to where his children are in bed.*)

STEPMOTHER (*quietly, like a vow*). You little brats, you think this is bad, but this is only the beginning . . . Oh yes, I'm going to get you . . . To fly, to fly . . . (*Eats hungrily, like a savage animal.*)

FATHER sits by his children's bed, but they turn away from him.

FATHER. I hate to be angry . . . And I hate to be poor . . . Here, take this bread . . . (*They still don't turn towards him, and he leaves the bread on their bed.*) What can I do? I work all the hours God gives me . . . Alright, don't speak . . . (*Stands to go.*) Goodnight . . .

GRETEL (*relenting*). We know how hard you work.

FATHER. Eat your bread . . . Go on . . . (*They eat hungrily.*) I know it sometimes doesn't seem like it, but I'm on your side . . . Always and always . . . Goodnight, then . . .

HANSEL. Don't go, father . . .

GRETEL. Not without making your silly face.

FATHER. I'm not in any mood for silly faces . . .

HANSEL. Please, please . . .

FATHER. I'm too tired . . .

GRETEL. Please, father . . .

He makes his silly face and the children laugh, prompting another sillier face. He tickles them, laughs with them, embraces them.

FATHER. Now, finish your bread, and off to sleep . . .

HANSEL. Say her rhyme first.

GRETEL. Say our mother's rhyme . . .

FATHER. Very well . . . Close your eyes. (*They close their eyes.*)

Life is hard and sometimes sore,
But I love you now and forevermore.
And even if I'm dead and gone,
I'll still be watching, willing you on.

Goodnight . . . (*Covers them with the blanket.*)

HANSEL *and* GRETEL (*in unison*). Goodnight, father.

FATHER *goes to table.* HANSEL *and* GRETEL *lie in bed, eating their bread contentedly. The* STEPMOTHER *cuts bread and cheese for* FATHER.

STEPMOTHER. Eat, while you can . . . There's hardly a crust left in the house.

FATHER (*picking at the food without appetite*). We can't go on . . . How can we feed our children, when we haven't enough to feed ourselves?

STEPMOTHER. Those children will eat us out of house and home . . . If only there was just the two of us.

FATHER. What do you mean?

HANSEL *and* GRETEL *have crept out of bed, and are listening closely.*

STEPMOTHER. Listen, and I'll tell you . . . Early in the morning we'll lead them deep into the forest, and leave them there so they'll never be able to find their way home again. (GRETEL *covers her ears, cuddles against* HANSEL *who continues to listen.*)

FATHER. Never! Wolves and bears will tear them to pieces!

STEPMOTHER. Would you rather they died slowly here of hunger? Is that what you want?

FATHER. No, but to leave them all alone in the wood, I could never do that.

STEPMOTHER. Then, it's simple, all four of us will die of hunger! Start making the coffins now, go on, two big and two small, for they'll be needed soon enough!

FATHER. Quiet! I can't think . . . (*Pushes food away.*) I can't eat . . . I'll go off my head . . .

STEPMOTHER. Oh, my poor love . . . You're tired . . . Come to bed, come on . . . (*Puts her arm around him.*) You know I'm right . . . Leave them in the forest . . . (*He starts to protest.*) Sssh, now, it's for the best, you'll see . . . In the morning we'll leave them . . . Trust me . . . Come on with me, my dear . . . My poor, dear love . . . (*She leads him off*).

GRETEL *cries against* HANSEL*'s shoulder. He strokes her hair gently.*

HANSEL. Don't cry, sister . . .

GRETEL. Did you hear?

HANSEL. I heard, sssh now . . . What good are tears?

GRETEL (*wiping her eyes*). I know, I know, they just make your face wet . . . But I'm so frightened . . . To leave us all alone in the forest . . . Horrible!

HANSEL. You won't be alone, Gretel . . . I'll look after you . . . (*Starts to go.*) Just be glad you've got such a brave and clever brother.

GRETEL. Ha-ha, so you say . . . Where are you going?

HANSEL. Outside . . . {*She starts to ask questions.*) Quiet, they'll hear us . . . I've got an idea . . . She's no match for us . . . (*Goes outside.*)

GRETEL. What are you doing?

HANSEL. Never mind . . . Go to sleep . . . (*Begins to fill his pockets with pebbles.*) Look at the moon . . . It's wearing a smile on its face, I'm sure of it . . . It knows we won't come to any harm.

GRETEL. Do you promise?

HANSEL. I promise . . . Go to sleep . . .

GRETEL (*lies back*). I'm so glad of you, Hansel . . . So glad . . .

She sleeps. HANSEL *continues to gather pebbles until the sun chases the moon out of the sky.*

Scene Three

The Wild Forest. Birdsong. Enter FATHER, *carrying his axe, followed by* GRETEL.

FATHER. Come on, girl, try and keep up!

GRETEL. I am trying. We've walked so far and my feet are sore.

FATHER. We're nearly there.

Enter STEPMOTHER, *calling off to* HANSEL.

STEPMOTHER. Move yourself, boy, you're slowing us down!

GRETEL (*to* FATHER). Why have we come so far?

FATHER. Don't bother me with your questions. Keep up. (*Goes.*)

GRETEL (*calls off*). Father? (STEPMOTHER *smiles at her.*) Hansel, are you there?

HANSEL (*as he enters*). I'm here, Gretel, it's alright . . . On you go.

GRETEL *follows* FATHER.

STEPMOTHER. Why are you always stopping and looking back in that idiotic fashion?

HANSEL. I'm trying to see the little white bird that sits on the chimney of our house.

STEPMOTHER. You stupid boy, we've come far too far to see the house! Move yourself, move your idle bones! (*He goes.*) Vile brat. (*Follows him off.*)

Enter FATHER *and* GRETEL.

FATHER. We've come far enough. You can play here while we go into the forest and chop wood . . .

STEPMOTHER (*as she enters*). And when we're ready, I'll come and get you . . . (*Calls after* HANSEL.) Hurry up, boy! (*Enter* HANSEL *looking back the way he came.*) Why are you always stopping and starting?

HANSEL. Wouldn't you like to know? Well, father, isn't it time you got to work? (*His* FATHER *can't look at him.*)

STEPMOTHER. Yes, you're quite right. (*To* FATHER.) To work, to work.

HANSEL. Goodbye, father. (*But his* FATHER *can't move.*)

STEPMOTHER. Well, what are you waiting for?

GRETEL. Don't worry, Father, we'll be alright . . . (*He goes without a word.*) Goodbye . . .

STEPMOTHER. Now see and behave yourselves! (*With a smile.*) We won't be far. (*Goes.*)

HANSEL. Gone . . .

GRETEL. Gone . . . Do you think they really will leave us behind?

HANSEL (*sits on ground*). Even if they do, I'll get you home.

GRETEL. But how? Tell me.

HANSEL. I just will. Trust me.

The sound of an axe chopping wood.

GRETEL. Listen! Father's axe . . . It's good to know he's close by. (*Sits, leans against his back.*)

HANSEL (*looking up*). Look how high the trees are.

GRETEL (*looking up*). They go all the way up to the clouds . . . Makes me dizzy.

HANSEL. Maybe we should live in the forest.

GRETEL. Don't be stupid.

HANSEL. It's not stupid . . . There's food all around, and water everywhere . . . (*Drinks from pool.*) Taste it, go on. (*Cups water in his hands, and* GRETEL *drinks from his hands.*) It tastes of earth and sky . . .

GRETEL. And leaves and rain . . . It's lovely . . .

HANSEL. In the day we could climb and swim and play . . .

GRETEL. And at night we could light a fire . . .

HANSEL. I'd make spears and we'd go hunting for food.

GRETEL (*shivers*). I'd like to be brave . . .

HANSEL. I'll show you how . . . I'm not afraid of anything . . .

A fierce voice comes from the trees.

VOICE. Who dares to walk in my forest?

HANSEL (*starting with fright*). Who's that?

GRETEL. It sounds like a giant!

VOICE. Let me see you! Let me look at you!

HANSEL. He's getting closer!

GRETEL. Hold my hand . . .

Enter ORIN, *more like a ragged beggar now than a Faerie-King.*

ORIN (*to* HANSEL). Are you he? Let me look at you! Are you my son?

HANSEL. Stay back, or I'll fight you!

GRETEL. He's not a giant.

HANSEL. He's just a funny old man.

ORIN (*disappointed*). You're not my son for he was brave and strong, and would not speak so rudely to a stranger.

GRETEL. He didn't mean to be rude.

ORIN (*lost in his own thoughts*). My son is lost . . . I have searched from the winter snow to the summer sun, and still he is lost to me . . .

GRETEL (*tentatively*). Don't be sad . . .

HANSEL. If he's lost, we'll help you find him . . .

ORIN. I am Faerie-King, and take help from no-one!

GRETEL. Now you're angry.

ORIN. I'm sorry . . . You are kind, but you must leave my forest.

HANSEL. Your forest?

ORIN. I may be poor and weak now, but there was a time . . . (HANSEL *sniggers*. ORIN *speaks sharply*.) You don't believe me?

GRETEL. I believe you . . .

ORIN. Thank you, little girl . . . (*Bows and smiles*.) But you must go now. Hurry!

HANSEL. Why can't we stay here with you?

ORIN. Listen to me! On Halloween a great evil broke its chains and escaped into our world. It took my son, and with him, my power and strength . . .

HANSEL. We could live in the forest.

ORIN. The forest is not as it was! The animals hide in fear, and even the great trees bow their heads . . . Go now! I warn you, this is not a safe place . . . Heed my words! (*Goes*.)

HANSEL. Wait . . . The Faerie-King? He's cracked.

GRETEL. I believe him.

HANSEL. Then you're cracked.

GRETEL (*with sudden urgency*). I want to go home . . . Go and bring father . . . Please, Hansel, I mean it . . . Go on!

HANSEL. I'm going, I'm going, keep your hair on . . . (*Goes*.)

GRETEL. A great evil . . . (*Shivers*.) I can't see it, but I know it's there, watching and waiting, waiting and watching . . . (*The sound of the axe ceases*.) Father's coming . . . I'll take his hand and we'll walk home together . . . All the way home . . . (*Enter* HANSEL.) Hansel? Where's father?

HANSEL. He's gone . . .

GRETEL. He can't be, I heard his axe.

HANSEL (*holds up a block of wood and some string*). This was tied to a branch . . . The wind banged it against the tree so that it sounded like an axe, and all the time they were gone . . . (*Throws block of wood away.*)

GRETEL. That was her idea, it must have been!

HANSEL. Come on, I'll take you home.

GRETEL. Oh yes, as quick as you can.

HANSEL. Now which way was it again?

GRETEL. Don't play the fool!

HANSEL. I thought I knew . . .

GRETEL. Hansel, I'm warning you!

HANSEL (*laughs, takes her hand*). On the way here, every time I stopped, I marked the way by dropping a white pebble from my pocket . . . There's one there, see, and another one there . . .

GRETEL. We can follow them home!

HANSEL. Easy.

GRETEL. My clever brother.

HANSEL. All the way home we'll think of her face when she sees us.

GRETEL. I can see it now. Her eyes will pop out her head. She'll be sick.

HANSEL. She thinks she's so clever . . . I'll show her who's clever, I'll show her . . . (*Exeunt.*)

Scene Four

FATHER's *cottage. The table is set for two. The*
STEPMOTHER *lights a candle on the table, makes herself*
pretty. She looks into a hand-mirror, fixes her hair. The sound
of the mirror cracking. She hides the mirror away. Enter
FATHER.

STEPMOTHER. Come and eat, dear husband.

FATHER. How can I eat?

STEPMOTHER. Look at all we have now there's just the two
of us.

FATHER. Oh yes, there's food on the table, but I've no
appetite for it.

STEPMOTHER. Go on, try some.

FATHER. I'll never eat again.

STEPMOTHER. Just a little piece . . . (*A knock at the door.*)
Who could that be?

FATHER (*hopefully*). The children!

STEPMOTHER. How can it be, you stupid man? (*He gets to*
his feet, goes to the door.) We'll never see them again.
(*Laughs.*) It can't be them, it can't possibly be . . .
(FATHER *lets in* HANSEL *and* GRETEL.) The children!

FATHER *sweeps the children up into his arms.*

FATHER. My beloved children . . . How happy I am to see
you . . .

STEPMOTHER (*recovering*). You wicked, wicked children!
Why did you stay so long in the wood? We've been worried
sick.

GRETEL. You were never worried!

HANSEL. But you're sick now! (*Laughs with* GRETEL.)

STEPMOTHER. I see your little adventure has done nothing to improve your manners.

GRETEL. What's the matter, stepmother? You don't look very pleased to see us.

STEPMOTHER. Pleased? Of course I'm pleased, you little . . . (*Barely controls her violent temper.*) dear. But we're still as poor as poor can be. So don't think you've come back to a slap-up feed! Don't think you can just walk in here and stuff your faces!

GRETEL. We're home again.

HANSEL. The food doesn't matter.

STEPMOTHER. You won't say that when you've gone a few days with nothing inside you! You'll change your tune then!

FATHER. Enough! (*To* GRETEL.) You're shivering.

GRETEL. I'm cold.

HANSEL. And I'm so sleepy.

FATHER (*breaking a loaf into two*). Take this, and off to bed where it's warm. (*Gives them bread, and chases them in a good-humoured way.*) Come on, to bed, the pair of you . . . Shoo, scat, vamoose . . . (HANSEL *evades* FATHER *who catches* GRETEL *instead and carries her to bed.*)

HANSEL (*to* STEPMOTHER, *with a cheeky wave*). Night, night, mummy. (*She goes to kill him, but* FATHER *returns to chase* HANSEL *to bed.*)

STEPMOTHER. Night-night, my dear. (HANSEL *appals her with a kiss, enjoys the fact that she is forced to return it.* FATHER *chases him to bed. The* STEPMOTHER, *shaken by a spasm of ill-will, speaks quietly to herself.*) I was always going to get them, but now I'm really going to get them! Oh to bite, and scratch, and tear! (*Eats hungrily, like a starving animal.*)

FATHER (*sitting by his children's bed*). It's good to have you home . . . I thought I'd lost you . . .

HANSEL. You'll never lose us, father . . .

GRETEL. No matter what, you'll never lose us.

FATHER. Welcome home . . . Sleep safe and warm in your bed tonight . . . Goodnight, Hansel. (*Kisses him.*) Goodnight, Gretel. (*Kisses her.*)

HANSEL *and* GRETEL (*in unison*). Goodnight, father.

FATHER *goes to table.* HANSEL *and* GRETEL *lie in bed and eat their bread.*

STEPMOTHER. So that's it then, is it? We may as well just lie down and die. There's hardly a mouthful to eat in the whole house!

FATHER. Then we'll share the last mouthful with the children.

HANSEL *and* GRETEL *listen closely.*

STEPMOTHER. Soon we'll be four skeletons sat round the table. A fine family we'll be then! No, husband, let us take them even deeper into the wood, so they'll never find their way out. (GRETEL *covers her ears, trying in vain to block her hearing, cuddles against* HANSEL.)

FATHER. No!

STEPMOTHER. And how are you going to feed them and take care of them? Tell me that!

FATHER. I have no answer.

STEPMOTHER. Then better to leave them to the forest.

FATHER. Perhaps the wild forest will care for them better than I . . .

STEPMOTHER. Of course it will! How clever you are, my dear.

FATHER. And perhaps they will find their own way in the world . . . Do you think that's possible?

STEPMOTHER. Oh yes, such strong and clever children are bound to find their own way . . . So put your mind to rest . . . Come and sleep, my clever husband . . . Tomorrow we'll take them deeper into the wood, and everything will be alright . . . You'll see, you'll see . . . (*Leads him off.*)

GRETEL. She's done it again!

HANSEL. Don't worry about her, Gretel . . . It's easy . . . I'm
far cleverer than her, even if she is a grown-up . . .
Goodnight.

GRETEL. Aren't you going to gather pebbles and tell me if the
moon is smiling?

HANSEL. I don't need to . . . I've got a much better idea.

GRETEL. What is it?

HANSEL. Never mind . . . (*Laughs quietly.*) Our stepmother is
so stupid. (*Holds bread up and crumbles small pieces into
his mouth.*) I'll take care of you, just you wait and see.

GRETEL. Do you promise?

HANSEL. Why should I bother? Or have you forgotten that
I'm the bravest and cleverest brother in the whole world?

GRETEL (*sleepily*). You are brave . . . and clever . . .

HANSEL. Well, then.

GRETEL. I'll help you . . . If I can . . . (*Sleeps.*)

HANSEL. I don't need help from anyone . . . Go to sleep, little
sister . . . Go to sleep . . . (*Laughs and drops some crumbs
into his mouth, like a baby bird taking food from his mother.*)

Scene Five

Birdsong. The wild forest. Enter FATHER, *carrying his axe,
followed by* GRETEL.

FATHER. Come on, girl, keep up.

GRETEL. We've come so much further this time . . .

FATHER. We'll stop here . . . Look, there's wood for a fire . . .
(*Begins to gather wood.*)

GRETEL. The forest is so huge . . . It goes on forever . . .
(*Shivers.*)

FATHER. Don't be frightened . . . Come and help. (*She helps
him gather wood.*)

Enter STEPMOTHER, *calling off to* HANSEL.

STEPMOTHER. You stupid boy, always looking back like that.
(*Enter* HANSEL.) What do you think you're playing at?

HANSEL (*smiling at* GRETEL). I've told you, I'm waving to
the little white bird that flies above our house. (FATHER
lights fire.)

STEPMOTHER (*witheringly*). What little bird? And besides
your house is far, far away, little boy.

HANSEL. I don't care . . . (*To* FATHER.) Why are you
lighting a fire?

FATHER. You've bread to eat, and a fire to keep you warm . . .

HANSEL. Are you going to leave us?

GRETEL. Are you?

STEPMOTHER. Leave your father alone! He's got work to do.

GRETEL. Father?

FATHER. You're good children . . . Brave and strong . . . Good
children . . . (*Goes.*)

STEPMOTHER (*with a cheery laugh*). Time to be going . . .
(*They gaze at her fiercely.*) Why are you staring at me like
that? Stop it at once!

GRETEL. We know all about you.

HANSEL. We know how cruel and horrible you are.

GRETEL (*indicates* AUDIENCE). And they know too . . .
They know you're going to leave us here.

HANSEL. And they know it was all your idea.

STEPMOTHER. Stop staring at me, you little brats! (*The
birdsong grows louder.*)

GRETEL. We're watching you! Even when you turn your back and leave us all alone, we'll be watching you as you walk away! (*Begins to chant and point accusingly.*) You're a witch, a witch, a witch-witch-witch!

STEPMOTHER (*squirming*). No! Stop it!

HANSEL (*to* AUDIENCE). Shout with us.

The AUDIENCE *chant and point along with* HANSEL *and* GRETEL.

HANSEL *and* GRETEL (*in unison with* AUDIENCE). You're a witch, a witch, a witch-witch-witch!

STEPMOTHER (*seems to wither and bend, covering her ears*). Stop it, you little brats! Oh, my head, my poor head!

HANSEL *and* GRETEL (*with* AUDIENCE.) You're a witch, a witch, a witch-witch-witch!

STEPMOTHER (*slyly, urgently*). Look! Up there! (*Points up into the trees.*) Everyone look! (*Silence as everyone looks.*) High up in the sky . . . Isn't that your little white bird? (*Vanishes into the trees.*)

HANSEL (*searching the sky*). Where?

GRETEL. There are lots and lots of birds, but I can't see a white one . . . (*They look at each other, understanding how they have been tricked, then look back for their* STEPMOTHER.)

HANSEL. Gone!

GRETEL. She's worse than a snake.

HANSEL. I won't let her bite you.

GRETEL (*suddenly excited*). Hansel, let's really show her this time!

HANSEL. Out with it! What's the plan?

GRETEL. Take me home now, straight away! That way we'll be back before her.

HANSEL. Genius!

GRETEL (*in ecstacy*). Oh Hansel, can you see her face when she walks in to find us home already?

HANSEL. I can see it now! (*Welcomes* GRETEL *as* STEPMOTHER.) Come in, dear stepmother.

GRETEL (*as* STEPMOTHER, *screams, takes a dizzy turn*). My head, my poor head . . . What are you doing here, you horrible little brats?

HANSEL. It's our home, in case you haven't noticed.

GRETEL. But it's impossible! How did you find your way?

HANSEL. We know more than you think! (STEPMOTHER *holds her stomach, mimes sickness.*) You look sick, stepmother, what a shame. Never mind, here's a bucket to catch it in. (STEPMOTHER *is hugely sick into imaginary bucket.* HANSEL *holds his nose, prepares to throw contents of bucket back over her.*)

GRETEL. Don't you dare, you vile little worm!

HANSEL. It's yours, so you can have it back!

GRETEL. I'll break every bone in your . . . (HANSEL *throws contents over* STEPMOTHER, *then embraces his sister, laughs with her.*) Oh, I can't wait . . . Take me home now!

HANSEL. Yes, come on . . . (*Stops in his tracks.*) I can't see my way.

GRETEL (*warningly*). It wasn't funny the first time!

HANSEL (*searching the ground*). I'm not joking . . . I can't find my path.

GRETEL. Stop it . . .

HANSEL (*still searching*). I wish I could . . . I'm sure I dropped some bread here . . .

GRETEL. Bread?

HANSEL. I broke my bread into pieces and used the crumbs to mark my way . . .

GRETEL. Then look harder . . . (*Helps him search.*) They must still be here . . . They must be . . . (*They look at each other, suddenly aware of the birdsong.*) Listen . . . The birds!

HANSEL. They've eaten the bread-crumbs . . . They've stolen my way home!

GRETEL. We'll never find our way now! If only you'd thought more carefully! Why didn't you think?

HANSEL. I did think!

GRETEL. It looks like it, and I thought you were meant to be clever!

HANSEL. At least I had an idea! What did you do? (*Imitates her cruelly.*) 'Help me, Hansel . . . Take me home, Hansel . . . '

GRETEL. I'd have thought of something if I'd known you were going to be so stupid!

HANSEL. Cry, cry, cry, that's all you do!

GRETEL. That's not true!

HANSEL (*imitates her again*). 'Help me . . . Hold my hand . . . '

GRETEL. Big-head!

HANSEL. Baby!

GRETEL. Know-all!

HANSEL. Cry-baby!

GRETEL. Stupid, that's all you are! A stupid little boy!

HANSEL. And you're . . . You're . . . (*Near to tears.*)

GRETEL (*seeing how near tears are*). Don't cry, Hansel. Please don't cry.

HANSEL (*through a mist of tears*). I never cry!

GRETEL. I know you don't . . . (*Embraces him.*) I know you don't.

HANSEL. I'm sorry . . .

GRETEL. We'll find another way, you'll see . . . (*The birdsong ceases abruptly.*) Listen, the birds have gone quiet.

HANSEL. Someone's coming!

GRETEL. Quickly, hide!

They hide. Enter ORIN, *who shivers by the fire.* HANSEL *arms himself with a stick.*

ORIN (*without looking around*). You won't hurt me with a stick. Come here where I can see you.

GRETEL. I know you.

HANSEL. It's that funny old man.

GRETEL (*correcting him, by way of an apology to* ORIN). The Faerie-King!

ORIN. So deep in the forest . . . Foolish children! I have told you – this is not a safe place . . . Go home.

HANSEL. We can't.

GRETEL. We've lost our way.

ORIN. Then you'd better find it again! In this forest there hides a great evil . . .

GRETEL. Stop it, please! You're only frightening us.

ORIN. I'm sorry, little girl . . . Evil grows stronger by the fear it inspires . . . So you must not be afraid.

GRETEL. Sometimes I am afraid of every sound and shadow.

ORIN. That is how fear serves us – it always sides with the thing we are afraid of.

GRETEL. Then I will try not to be afraid.

ORIN. Good girl . . . I must go now . . . (*Staggers.*)

GRETEL. What's the matter? Are you ill?

HANSEL. Come closer to the fire. (*They help him.*)

GRETEL. You're shivering.

HANSEL. Pardon me for asking, but have you found your son? (ORIN *shakes his head.*) I'm sorry.

ORIN. The witch has great power and has hidden him where my eyes cannot see.

GRETEL. The witch!

ORIN. I'm frightening you again, forgive me.

HANSEL. We're used to witches . . . You must be hungry.

GRETEL. Here, take this bread. (*Offers her bread.*)

ORIN. It's all you have.

HANSEL. Take it.

ORIN (*takes bread, cherishes it*). Then perhaps it's true.

GRETEL. What's true?

ORIN. There is no magic can match the kindness of a child's heart.

GRETEL. We know that food has to be shared, that's all.

ORIN. Then you know all you need . . . (*Gives back bread.*) Your kindness makes me strong . . . Thank you. (*Goes to leave.*)

HANSEL. Don't go . . .

ORIN. I must find my son.

GRETEL. Don't leave us alone . . .

ORIN. Remember – you must not be afraid. (*Goes.*)

HANSEL. Everyone leaves us . . .

GRETEL. Everyone . . . Come over to the fire.

HANSEL (*shivers*). I've never felt so alone . . .

GRETEL. Listen to the wind in the trees . . . It feels like we're the only people left in the world.

The sudden sound of a horn and a parade drum. Enter a group of ragged circus people – SHOES, *a clown, who plays the horn and drum, followed by* RAB, *an acrobat/trapeze flyer, and* MOFF, *a bareback rider.*

RAB. Roll up, roll up!

MOFF. Come and see The Magic Circus – The Greatest Show On Earth!

RAB. Roll up, roll up!

MOFF. Well, well, what have we here?

RAB. Come on, little boy, and you, little girl. Step right this way! (HANSEL *and* GRETEL *step back from him.*)

MOFF. Well, aren't you coming?

GRETEL (*stunned*). N – no, thank you.

RAB. You're not scared of us?

MOFF. We don't want anyone who's scared.

HANSEL. I'm not scared.

MOFF (*to* HANSEL). What's your name?

HANSEL. Hansel, and this is my sister, Gretel.

MOFF. Names are so stupid . . . I, for instance, am Moff.

RAB. The best and bravest bareback rider in all the world! (MOFF *bows grandly.*) And I, for instance, am her brother Rab.

MOFF. The greatest acrobat who ever lived! (RAB *bows grandly.*) And this is Uncle Shoes. (SHOES *goes to shake their hands.*)

GRETEL. You're a clown.

SHOES (*stops in his tracks*). I beg your pardon!

GRETEL. Well, you are, aren't you?

SHOES (*outraged*). Just because I've got big shoes and a funny face, you think I'm a clown.

GRETEL. Yes.

SHOES. And I suppose you think I'm wearing huge spotty pants under my trousers?

GRETEL (*laughing*). Yes.

SHOES (*a plea from the heart*). Nothing could be further from the truth! Can no-one understand that I'm an enormously important man? A lawyer! A doctor! A prime minister! A headmaster! (*His trousers fall down to reveal his huge spotty pants.*) It can't be helped . . . Pleased to meet you, Hansel and Gretel . . . (*Shakes hands, becomes entangled, unable to get both hands free at once.*) Help me! Someone help! (MOFF *and* RAB *try to separate them, but they become entangled in an endlessly changing web of handshakes, and they all fall to the ground in a heap.*) Oh dear, if this is hullo, what's goodbye going to be like? (*A command.*) Everyone (*Thinks.*) . . . has an itchy nose! (*All rub their itchy noses, and have thus reclaimed their hands.*) Miraculo! Works every time.

HANSEL. I like you . . . You're funny.

SHOES. And would you like to be funny, young man?

HANSEL. Will you teach me?

SHOES. Of course I will, but you'll have to come with us . . .

HANSEL. I don't know . . .

GRETEL. What's a circus doing in the middle of the forest?

SHOES (*sawing the air*). They don't trust us! Oh, mournful day! (*Weeps into hanky, wrings out a stream of water, laughs with* HANSEL.)

GRETEL. I was wondering, that's all.

RAB. We're passing through, Gretel, on our way to all the great and far countries of the world.

GRETEL. All of them?

MOFF. All.

GRETEL. That sounds wonderful.

RAB. It is . . . More wonderful than you can dream of . . . And what, for instance, are you doing in the middle of the forest?

GRETEL. Well, you see, for instance, we're . . . we're . . . (*Hesitates.*)

MOFF. Spill the beans!

RAB. Spit it out!

HANSEL (*blaming himself*). We're lost.

RAB (*laughing*). That's not very good, is it?

MOFF (*laughing*). You haven't done very well, have you?

SHOES. Pay no attention to them . . . They think they know
everything just because they're beautiful . . . (*Kindly, to*
HANSEL *and* GRETEL.) You have to be lost if you want to
find yourself . . . Isn't that right?

HANSEL. I suppose so.

SHOES. There you are, then.

RAB. So come with us! (*Kneels to* GRETEL.) I'll teach you to
tumble and then to fly with me on the high trapeze . . .
We'll be two birds diving and soaring . . . I'll never let you
fall.

MOFF (*kneels to* HANSEL). And I'll teach you to ride my
great white horses . . . You'll be a king riding to war, and
I'll be your queen . . . How the crowds will cheer and cheer!

SHOES. And don't forget the clowning! I'll teach you all my
tricks.

HANSEL. I want to learn everything!

SHOES. Good boy! Come on with your Uncle Shoes!
(HANSEL *goes to him happily, but sees that* GRETEL *has
not moved.*)

HANSEL. Gretel?

GRETEL (*quietly*). No.

RAB. What did you say?

GRETEL (*more firmly*). I'm not coming.

RAB. But why?

GRETEL. We may be lost, but our father knows where we
are . . . He'll come for us, I know he will.

MOFF *and* SHOES (*in unison*). Hansel?

HANSEL (*goes to* GRETEL*'s side*). I could never leave her . . .
I'm sorry.

MOFF. We have a father too . . . He's The Strong Man in the
circus . . . He'll look after you . . . He's not scared of
anything . . . (*Suddenly holds her side as if in pain, gives a
little cry of grief.* UNCLE SHOES *puts his arm around her.*)

HANSEL. What is it, Moff? What's the matter?

MOFF. Nothing . . . (*Recovers.*) My heart . . . I so much
wanted you to come . . . Won't you change your mind?

GRETEL (*shaking her head*). Our father will come for us.

RAB. But what if some-*thing* else comes first?

GRETEL. Some-*thing*?

MOFF. Oh yes, this forest is full of demons and monsters.

GRETEL. Don't, please!

RAB. Have you never, for instance, heard of The Mad Monk?
(UNCLE SHOES *hides in terror against* MOFF.)

HANSEL. No, never.

SHOES. J-just hearing his name makes my legs turn to water.
The Mad Monk! (*His legs turn to water, can hardly hold his
weight.*)

MOFF. He's the fiercest of all the forest's creatures!

RAB. He'll snap your bones like twigs and use them to thatch
the roof of his house! (GRETEL *covers her ears.*)

HANSEL (*uncertain*). You're teasing us . . . (RAB *and* MOFF
and SHOES *shake their heads.*) Say you are . . .

A strange, chattering cry is heard from high in the trees.

SHOES. That's his cry!

RAB. He's coming!

SHOES. Help, help! (*Runs hopelessly in all directions, stops,
resigns himself to his fate.*) There's no escape. He's coming!

MOFF (*to* HANSEL *and* GRETEL). There's nothing you can do! (HANSEL *and* GRETEL *huddle together, covering their eyes.*) The Mad Monk is coming!

MONKEY, *a monkey-creature, clad perhaps in waistcoat and bell-hop hat, swings down from the trees.*

RAB (*shouting, throwing his arms open in welcome*). Monkey! Over here, you mad wee man!

MONKEY *runs to him, jumps into his arms, and tumbles with him, before jumping on* MOFF *and* SHOES. HANSEL *and* GRETEL *uncover their eyes and watch with delight.*

GRETEL (*laughing*). So he's The Mad Monk?

HANSEL. He's brilliant!

MOFF. Go on, Monkey, go and say hullo to Hansel and Gretel.

SHOES. On you go, boy . . . (MONKEY *hides behind* SHOES.)

GRETEL. Look, he's shy . . .

HANSEL. Come on, we won't hurt you . . . (MONKEY *approaches cautiously.*)

GRETEL (*patting her knees*). Come on, boy . . . (MONKEY *breaks into a run, and goes to her, chattering playfully.*) Quiet, now! You've said hullo, so now you can calm down . . . (MONKEY *calms down.*) That's a good boy. (MONKEY *leaps at* HANSEL.)

HANSEL (*spinning* MONKEY *around playfully*). Is he a monkey or is he a boy? (MONKEY *lets go, ceases playing.*)

RAB (*shrugs*). Neither . . . Both . . . He's a monkey-boy.

MOFF. The circus pet.

GRETEL. Can he talk? (MONKEY *chatters.*) Yes, I know you can, but can you talk like we talk? *(*MONKEY *chatters.*)

SHOES. That's all you'll get from him . . . But he's the greatest fun . . . Do you like him?

GRETEL. He's lovely . . . But he has sad eyes . . .

MOFF. He could be your pet too.

SHOES. Won't you change your mind?

MOFF (*to* HANSEL).
    If I were a Queen
    What would I do?
    I'd make you King
    And I'd wait for you.

RAB (*to* GRETEL).
    If I were a King
    What would I do?
    I'd make you Queen
    For I'd marry you.

    Come with us, Gretel.

MOFF. Come with us, Hansel.

SHOES. Come with us to all the far countries of the world.

HANSEL. Gretel?

GRETEL. I'd like to . . . I'd really like to . . . . (HANSEL, SHOES, RAB *and* MOFF *begin to cheer, but* MONKEY *leaps at* GRETEL, *shaking his head and chattering urgently.*) What is it, Monkey?

MOFF (*pulling* MONKEY *away*). Never mind him!

GRETEL. He doesn't want us to come.

RAB (*angrily, to* MONKEY). You stupid Monkey! Go away! Go on!

GRETEL. Don't send him away . . .

MOFF (*to* MONKEY). Leave us! Go on! You're not wanted! (MONKEY *goes sadly.*)

GRETEL. Poor Monkey . . .

RAB. Don't feel sorry for him . . . He was jealous, that's all . . .

MOFF. Jealous that we'd like you better than him . . . Come on, it's time to go!

RAB. Step right this way! (*But* GRETEL *does not move.*)
You're not coming, are you? (GRETEL *shakes her head.*)
I'd never let you fall . . .

HANSEL. Gretel . . .

GRETEL. No . . . (HANSEL *takes her by the arm, she shrugs him off.*) No!

RAB. Then we must leave you . . . Goodbye, Gretel.

MOFF. Goodbye, Hansel.

UNCLE SHOES *plays a sad note on his horn.*

RAB. Of course, Uncle Shoes – your horn! (*Takes pipes out of his pocket.*) Take these, Gretel, and if you do change your mind, blow them and Uncle Shoes will hear you and answer with his horn. (*He blows and* UNCLE SHOES *replies.*) That way you'll find us. Take them, please.

GRETEL (*taking the pipes*). Thank you, you're very kind.

MOFF. Try them. (GRETEL *blows the pipes and* SHOES *replies.*) Don't forget now, if your father doesn't come . . . (GRETEL *blows, but before* SHOES *can reply a bird sings from the trees.*)

GRETEL. Listen, a bird has answered me!

RAB *and* MOFF *begin to sing with mischievous charm.*

RAB *and* MOFF.
Do you ask what the birds say? The sparrow, the dove,
The linnet and thrush say, 'I love and I love!'
And the lark is so brimful of gladness and love,
The green fields below him, the blue sky above,
That he sings, and he sings – and forever sings he –
'I love my love, and my love loves me!'

RAB *and* MOFF *bow grandly, and go.*

SHOES. So it's farewell then, my fine new friends. (*He bows and his trousers fall down.*) Ah yes . . . It's a grand life if you don't weaken . . . Don't forget us, now . . . Don't forget . . . (*Goes, playing his horn and banging his drum.*)

HANSEL. One day . . . One day I want to be just like them.

GRETEL. I know.

HANSEL. And we could have gone with them but, oh no, we had to stay here!

GRETEL. I wanted to go too!

HANSEL. Then why didn't you? Stupid!

GRETEL. There's something . . . And father will come back for us.

HANSEL. So you say . . . Stuck in this place!

GRETEL. Come over to his fire . . . Don't be angry. (*Leads him to the fire.*) See how it burns still . . . Feel how warm it is.

HANSEL (*lying down*). It is warm . . . Makes me sleepy . . .

GRETEL. Then go to sleep . . . (*Lying down.*) Listen to the trees swaying in the wind, and go to sleep . . .

HANSEL (*sleepily*). Gretel?

GRETEL. What?

HANSEL. Will he come?

GRETEL. I know he will . . . If we believe, if we really believe.

HANSEL. How long must we wait?

GRETEL. I don't know, Hansel . . . (*Throws stick on fire.*) Until the fire goes out . . .

HANSEL. And then will you blow the pipes?

GRETEL. Go to sleep . . . (*He sleeps.*) And then I'll blow the pipes . . . (*Sleeps.*)

The fire burns gently, the wind sounds in the high branches.

FATHER (*from off*). Hansel, Gretel, are you there?

HANSEL (*dreamily*). Father?

Enter FATHER.

FATHER. I've found you . . . My children.

GRETEL (*dreamily*). I knew you'd come.

FATHER. Come on, up onto your feet . . . It's time you were on your way.

HANSEL. It's so warm here . . .

FATHER. To market, to market, to buy a fat pig.
Home again, home again, jiggity-jig.

Hurry now, lazybones! Everything's ready, and it's all for you . . . Your bed's made, the fire's lit and the table is covered with food . . . As much as you can eat . . .

GRETEL. We're coming, father . . . Come on, Hansel . . .

HANSEL. Here I come . . . (*They get slowly to their feet.*)

FATHER. Hurry up, the pair of you . . . Don't be slow . . . (*Vanishes.*)

GRETEL. We met circus people, father, a clown and a monkey-boy and . . . Father?

HANSEL. Father . . . He's gone . . .

GRETEL (*understanding*). He was never here . . . It was a dream . . . He never came back for us. (*They embrace.*) My brother . . .

HANSEL. My sister . . . The fire's almost out.

GRETEL (*takes out pipes*). Then it's time we were on our way . . . Are you ready?

HANSEL. I'm ready. (GRETEL *blows the pipes.*)

GRETEL (*listening keenly*). Nothing.

HANSEL. Blow harder. (*She blows again, and the answering horn can be heard in the distance.*)

GRETEL. It's Uncle Shoes! Did you hear?

HANSEL. I heard! This way.

GRETEL. No, this way! (*She blows again, listens to the distant horn.*) No, that way . . .

HANSEL. No, idiot, this way!

GRETEL. Oh dear, we can hear it, but we can't tell where it's coming from. (*A bird sings from the trees.*)

HANSEL. Look, Gretel, our little white bird . . . It's talking to you.

GRETEL. It's beautiful . . . It's flown away!

HANSEL. No, there it is, high on that branch.

GRETEL. It wants to show us the way . . . (*The horn sounds in the distance.*) It wants to show us the way . . . Quickly, then! (*They run off, following their white bird, and the sound of the distant horn.*)

Enter ORIN.

ORIN. Do not be afraid, little Hansel and Gretel. You must not be afraid for you have a courage in your hearts stronger than any power in this great forest. You are a match for anything, even the witch. By all the world's magic, even the witch! (*Goes.*)

FATHER (*from off*). Hansel, Gretel, are you there? (*Enter* FATHER.) Their fire! This is where I left them! But they've gone . . . Gone to find their own way. May this wild forest care for them better than I . . . And may my love and their mother's love burn bright inside them and keep them from harm . . . (*Kneels by fire.*)

Life is hard and sometimes sore,
But I love you now and forevermore,
And even if I'm dead and gone,
I'll still be watching, willing you on.

End of Act One.

ACT TWO

Scene One

A misty clearing deep in The Wild Forest. The sound of
GRETEL'*s pipes and, closer,* SHOES' *horn. Enter* RAB,
MOFF, MONKEY *and* UNCLE SHOES *at a run.*

MOFF. They're coming! They're really coming!

RAB. They're right behind us! Listen!

The sound of GRETEL'*s pipes, closer now.* UNCLE
SHOES *seems reluctant to reply.*

RAB. Uncle Shoes! (*But* SHOES *makes no move to reply.*
RAB *takes the horn and blows it.*) We must make them
welcome.

MOFF. You know we must, Uncle Shoes.

RAB. Come on!

MOFF (*to* MONKEY, *firmly*). And not a sound out of you!
(*They vanish into the mist.*)

Enter HANSEL *and* GRETEL.

HANSEL (*disappointed*). No-one!

GRETEL. And they sounded so close . . . Where's our little
white bird?

HANSEL. Up there! No, it's flown away.

GRETEL (*exhausted*). Into the mist.

HANSEL. Hurry, Gretel!

GRETEL (*sinks down*). I can't take another step.

HANSEL. We'll lose our bird . . . (*Pulls her by the arm.*) Up
onto your feet.

GRETEL. Leave me alone! You go if you want . . .

HANSEL. You can't just sit there.

GRETEL. Why not? We've walked for a night and a day and what have we found? Nothing! Nothing in the middle of nowhere!

MOFF, MONKEY, and UNCLE SHOES appear from the mist.

MOFF. This way . . . You've found us . . . Step right this way.

HANSEL. Moff, Monkey, Uncle Shoes! (MOFF *controls* MONKEY. UNCLE SHOES *cannot look at them.*)

MOFF. Look – It is your reward.

The mist clears to reveal a beautiful, magical gypsy fortune-teller's caravan made of food and sweets so delicious that the fragrance of ginger and cinnamon seems to hang tantalisingly in the air. Ragged tents form an encampment around the caravan. RAB swings above the encampment on a rope or trapeze hung from a high branch.

RAB. Welcome, Hansel and Gretel! Welcome to The Magic Circus!

MOFF.
  If I were a Queen
  What would I do?
  I'd make you King
  And I'd wait for you.

RAB.
  If I were a King
  What would I do?
  I'd make you Queen
  For I'd marry you.

HANSEL and GRETEL stare at the caravan in delight.

GRETEL. It's wonderful!

RAB. And it's all for you . . . It's all for you . . . Come closer . . .

HANSEL. The roof is made of sugar-loaf!

GRETEL. And look, Hansel, the walls are made from honey-cake!

MONKEY *runs at them, chattering, shaking his head.*
MOFF *takes hold of him.*

HANSEL. What is it, Monkey?

GRETEL. What's wrong with him?

RAB. I've told you, he's jealous, that's all.

MOFF. Go away, Monkey! If you can't be their friend, you
can't be our friend either . . . Go away! (MONKEY *flees
into the forest.*)

GRETEL (*suddenly alarmed*). Hansel, hold my hand.

HANSEL. It's all right, sister – look at the wheels – they're
made from the thickest chocolate!

GRETEL. And the windows, see how they sparkle! (*Touches
window, licks her finger.*) It's made of spun sugar!

HANSEL. And it smells so lovely . . . (*Breathes in deeply.*)
Ginger and cinnamon . . . It's a feast of everything we've
ever wanted!

GRETEL. I'm so hungry . . . You taste the wheel, I'll try a
piece of the roof. (*They eat hungrily.*) Oh, it's delicious . . .

HANSEL. I didn't know anything could taste so good . . .

A voice comes from inside the caravan.

VOICE. Tip-tap, tip-tap, who's that at my door?

SHOES. The wind, the wind, the child of heaven.

GRETEL. I heard a voice . . .

HANSEL. I don't care.

GRETEL. Perhaps we should stop . . . (*Keeps eating.*)

HANSEL. I can't stop . . . (*Keeps eating.*)

GRETEL. I know, neither can I . . .

VOICE.
    Nibble, nibble, little rat.
    It's my wheelie-house you're nibbling at.

GRETEL. I can't stop . . .

HANSEL (*quickly, as he guzzles*).
I'm a bird, and she's a mousey
Nibbling at your wheelie-housey.

They continue to eat hungrily. A light goes on in the caravan. HANSEL *and* GRETEL *don't notice, but* RAB, SHOES *and* MOFF *do, and they back slowly away from the caravan.*

GRETEL. Taste this . . . You must! (*She puts some sugar-loaf into* HANSEL'*s mouth.*)

HANSEL. Heaven . . . Try this. (*Puts some chocolate into her mouth.*)

GRETEL. Oh heaven . . .

The door opens and LA STREGAMAMA, *a kindly old Gypsy fortune-teller, who walks with the aid of a long stick, comes out of the caravan.*

STREGAMAMA. Good evening, my dears.

HANSEL *and* GRETEL *have started with fright.*

GRETEL. We're s-sorry . . .

HANSEL. We couldn't help it . . .

GRETEL. We're so hungry, and your house is so delicious . . .

STREGAMAMA (*laughs warmly*). Don't be frightened of La Stregamama. Take what you like. You're very welcome to my house. La Stregamama has been longing for little children to come into her heart and into her home. Oh my dears, you are so very welcome.

HANSEL. Do you mean it?

STREGAMAMA. Of course I do, my little darling.

Song – 'La Stregamama'.

STREGAMAMA.
Two little children alone in the wood,
Welcome to friendship and laughter and food.

Happiness waits through the marshmallow door,
Eat till you're egg-shaped, then ask for some more.

MOFF *and* RAB. La Stregamama, La Stregamama.

GRETEL. I'm too tired to argue, you seem very good.

HANSEL. And we're far from our home, and lost in the wood.

STREGAMAMA.
    The forest is icy, my blankets are warm,
    Marzipan curtains will keep out the storm.
    Two caravan children all cosy and fed,
    Tucked up and safe in a caravan bed.

MOFF *and* RAB. La Stregamama, La Stregamama.

GRETEL. We dream every bedtime of eating too much,

HANSEL. And now it's come true, a dream we can touch.

STREGAMAMA.
    Dreams spun like sugar, dreams you can smell,
    Dreams made of ginger and honey as well.
    Dreams that leave chocolate smeared on your cheek,
    Dreams about puddings that make your legs weak.

MOFF *and* RAB. La Stregamama, La Stregamama.

MOFF *and* RAB. Who'd roam the forest where the night
    frowns,

STREGAMAMA. When there is playtime and puddings and
    clowns?

MOFF *and* RAB. Who would be frightened and frozen and thin,

STREGAMAMA. When my gypsy caravan whispers 'come in'?

    End of song.

MOFF. Stay with us! Please stay!

RAB. Say you'll stay!

    HANSEL *nods eagerly and looks to* GRETEL.

GRETEL (*quickly*). We'll stay.

STREGAMAMA. Oh happy day.

HANSEL. I want to stay here forever and ever . . .

STREGAMAMA. And so you shall. Come now, you must be shown to your bed.

HANSEL. I'm so sleepy . . .

STREGAMAMA. This way, sweetie-pie . . . Your feather-bed is made up with the softest sheets, and in the morning you'll eat a breakfast of hot pancakes with sugar and apples . . . (*Leads him, followed by* GRETEL, *to a covered trailer near to her caravan.*) Off to bed, then, off we go . . . (*Suddenly she shoves* HANSEL *forward, clangs shut a door, and pulls away the trailer's cover to reveal* HANSEL *locked inside a circus lion's cage.*) I have him!

HANSEL. Where am I?

STREGAMAMA. Oh, I can taste him now, the sweetness.

HANSEL (*shaking the bars*). Let me out!

GRETEL. Taste him?

STREGAMAMA. Oh yes, I'm going to cook him up. Behold – (*Uncovers her soot-black oven built up against the side of the caravan.*) My roasting oven!

HANSEL. She's a witch!

GRETEL. No, it can't be true . . .

STREGAMAMA (*laughs, kisses her oven*). My roaring, roasting rascal-rogue. (*Luxuriates.*) Oh, we'll cook him! (*Polishes it adoringly with her sleeve.*)

HANSEL. It is true! Run, Gretel!

GRETEL (*confused and terrified*). Hansel . . .

HANSEL. Run!

STREGAMAMA (*joining in as if her life depended on it*). Run, Gretel! You've got to! Run!

HANSEL. Run!

STREGAMAMA. Run! (GRETEL *runs off.*) What a relief, my heart's pounding . . . I'm so glad the sweet little girlie has run away from the cruel and greedy witch. But do you think she's safe? No, she's not, is she? No . . . She's going to come back because she loves the little boy, and can't leave him all on his own. Here she comes, the angel . . . (*She laughs as* GRETEL *enters slowly, goes to the cage and embraces* HANSEL *through the bars.*) I love to use love against people – it is the blackest of my arts!

UNCLE SHOES *goes to* GRETEL *but can think of nothing to do or say.*

MOFF (*to* LA STREGAMAMA). Please, La Stregamama, we have done all you asked!

RAB. Please, La Stregamama!

STREGAMAMA. On your knees when you're speaking to me! (RAB *and* MOFF *kneel.* SHOES *falls to his knees before* GRETEL.) Better. Now, let me hear you beg.

RAB. We beg you, oh great one . . .

MOFF. We beg you to give us back our father.

RAB. You promised that if we brought another in his place you would spare him and set him free.

STREGAMAMA. Ah, but you know how I love to break promises.

RAB *and* MOFF (*in unison*). We beg you, great one.

STREGAMAMA. Mmmm, I'll have to think about it . . . Am I lovely?

RAB. You are lovelier than the moon that already climbs in the evening sky.

STREGAMAMA (*patting her long red hair*). And my hair – how does it shine?

MOFF. It shines brighter than the morning sun.

STREGAMAMA. It does, doesn't it, then know that I am pleased with you, my servants. (*Gestures, and the caravan door opens.*) I give you back your father. (LOB *the strong-man comes out of the caravan.*) You are free, strong-man.

(*Gestures and his bonds break loose.*) Your children have saved you.

RAB *and* MOFF *run into their father's arms.*

LOB. My beloved children . . . (*To* SHOES.) My brother.

SHOES (*sadly*). My brother. (*Joins the embrace.*)

LA STREGAMAMA *watches, moved by the reunion. Silence, save for the sound of* GRETEL *crying.*

STREGAMAMA (*with growing interest*). Is that tears I hear?

HANSEL (*comforting* GRETEL). Ssh, sister, shush now.

STREGAMAMA. I do so hope it is . . . (*Goes over to* GRETEL, *peers at her closely.*) I can't see any tears because my eyes are weak, but I can hear them and smell them. Let me wipe away your tears, my dear . . .

HANSEL. Leave her alone!

STREGAMAMA. Silence, brat! (*Gestures, and sends* HANSEL *crashing to the floor of his cage.*) Now, where was I? Ah, yes – your tears. (*Takes hold of* GRETEL *wipes away her tears carefully with her finger.*) I don't want to miss any. (*Licks her finger.*) Mm, dee-licious! I must have more! I must, I must! I'll cook him now, now . . . But I've forgotten . . . (*With heavy disappointment.*) I've already eaten . . .

MOFF, RAB *and* SHOES *look around apprehensively, checking that everyone's there.* SHOES *counts them all silently.*

RAB. I don't understand.

MOFF. How can you have eaten?

RAB. We're all here.

STREGAMAMA (*enjoying their puzzlement*). Are we?

SHOES (*looking at the cage*). Of course – the lion . . . She's eaten the lion.

STREGAMAMA (*burps*). Beg pardon.

SHOES. Poor old Leo . . . He was a great friend . . . (*Bows his head in solemn remembrance.*)

LOB (*with seething anger*). She takes everything!

STREGAMAMA (*sharply, making* LOB *start back in fear*). And why shouldn't I since I am the strongest of all! (*Gets back to the main problem.*) If only I hadn't had my tea . . . I know! I'll put my fingers down my throat, I'll sick up my tea, and then I'll have room to eat the boy straightaway. How clever I am! Fetch my bucket . . . (*Puts her fingers down her throat.*)

SHOES. No!

STREGAMAMA (*mid-retch*). What did you say?

SHOES. You c-can't eat him.

STREGAMAMA (*icily*). Have a care, clown, or I'll have you on the same dish!

SHOES. You can't eat him because . . . because . . .

STREGAMAMA (*glinting with menace*). Because why, exactly?

SHOES. Because he's so skinny and thin.

STREGAMAMA. Is he? (*Peers into cage.*)

SHOES. See for yourself . . . There's nothing of him.

MOFF (*catching on*). It's true – he's just skin and bone.

STREGAMAMA. This is bad news, very bad . . . But wait . . . He must be fattened up. (*Pokes* HANSEL *through the bars with her long stick.*) That's it! I'll feed him up till he's as fat as a prize pig. (*Pokes* HANSEL *some more.*) What do you think of that, my little shivery-bite?

Summoning all her courage, GRETEL *faces up to the crazy witch.*

GRETEL. Put that stick down and leave my brother alone!

STREGAMAMA (*utterly stunned*). What!!

GRETEL. You heard! Unlock that cage and let him out! Go on! You're cruel and ugly and horrible and I won't let you hurt him! Unlock the cage!

STREGAMAMA (*shaking in fear and haste*). At once, my dear. How fierce you are . . . (*Takes out the big key.*) And how right . . . I am so horrible . . . So good of you to point it out . . .

GRETEL. Hurry up!

STREGAMAMA (*fumbling with key at lock*). I'm hurrying, I'm hurrying!

GRETEL. We're not staying in this place! (*To* HANSEL.) Soon, you'll be free . . .

STREGAMAMA. Oh yes, soon, soon . . . (*Begins to laugh, holding her sides, pointing mockingly at* GRETEL.) You really thought I was going to let him out . . . Oh, it hurts, it hurts . . . You silly little fool, La Stregamama never lets anyone go!

GRETEL, *exhausted, sits by the caravan with her arms over her head.* LOB *rounds on the witch.*

LOB. Do what she says, witch! Let the boy go!

MOFF. No, father!

LOB. What freedom is this – to be slaves to a monster? I'll fight her!

STREGAMAMA. You dare to challenge me?

LOB. I challenge you!

LA STREGAMAMA *unleashes a bolt of fire from her fingertips which sends him to his knees.*

STREGAMAMA. The Strong-Man, ha! I have more strength in my little finger!

LOB. I am strong . . . (*Picks up huge hammer, gets to his feet, charges at her.*) I am strong!

She unleashes another bolt of fire, sending LOB *crashing to the ground.* MOFF, RAB *and* SHOES *rush to his side.*

STREGAMAMA. Come on, then! Come on! Who's next?
(*The circus people confront her angrily, but they look away
and hang their heads in defeat.*) No, I didn't think so.
(*Screeches triumphantly.*) Bolts of fire come flashing from
my fingertips! I can fly through the air like the mighty
eagle! I am queen of witches and no-one can stand against
me! (*Calms herself.*) And if I say the boy's to be fattened
up, then fattened up he will be! (*Loads a huge pile of food
from the caravan onto a tray.*) You wanted to eat, boy,
you wanted everything on a plate, well here it is! (*Opens
cage, puts in food, slams and locks door.*) There you are,
my dear – all you ever dreamed of . . . Well, what are you
waiting for? Eat, boy, stuff yourself!

HANSEL. I won't touch your food!

GRETEL. That's it, Hansel, not a single bite.

STREGAMAMA. How very rude, after all the trouble I've
gone to.

HANSEL. Keep your food! I won't touch it!

STREGAMAMA. We'll soon see about that. (*Casts spell – *)

Eat, my sweet, a witch's treat
To fill you up from head to feet.
Eat, I command it, eat, eat, eat!

HANSEL *goes slowly towards the food.*

GRETEL. No, Hansel, leave it alone!

HANSEL. I can't stop myself . . .

SHOES. She's put a spell on him.

STREGAMAMA (*laughing*). Eat up now, there's a good boy.

HANSEL (*begins to eat*). It tastes so lovely . . . Lovely . . .
(*Crams food into his mouth.*)

GRETEL (*reaching through bars*). Give it to me, I'll take it
away . . .

HANSEL. No, it's mine, mine! I want it all! You want it, but
you can't have it . . . It's mine, mine! (*Takes food into far
corner where he guzzles.*)

GRETEL. Oh Hansel . . . I can't bear to look. (SHOES *covers the cage.*)

STREGAMAMA (*like a proud housewife*). How pleased I am with my cruelty today . . . Everything's perfect. And now I think I'll have an early night, so I can work up a really good appetite for breakfast . . . I can hardly wait . . . (*To* GRETEL.) You won't run away, will you, girlie? No, you couldn't leave your brother. (*To circus people.*) And none of you will run away, will you, or I'll fly after you and bring you back to my roasting oven. You know I will. (*Yawns.*) So sleepy . . . I'll see how plump he is in the morning . . . (*Goes to caravan.*) I really should wash my hair . . . Goodnight one and all . . . Sweet dreams . . . (*Goes into caravan, closes door behind her.*)

The circus people are awkward in the face of GRETEL's *anger and grief.* SHOES *goes to her, performs a foolish trick, but it's hollow and joyless, and* GRETEL *turns away from him.*

LOB. We have done you such wrong, little girl . . . Such wrong . . .

RAB. We did what we had to!

MOFF. To save our father.

LOB. The witch has great power . . .

SHOES. Before she came it was we who were great! There were twenty clowns, there were fire-eaters, performing dogs, six lions and their tamer . . .

MOFF. And teams of beautiful white horses . . . So beautiful . . .

LOB. And there were musicians and knife throwers and trapeze-artists . . .

RAB. Acrobats, tightrope walkers, mechanics and engineers, the ringmaster, cooks and ticket-sellers, midgets, tall-men, wrestlers, jugglers . . . All gone . . .

LOB. One by one she has cooked them all in her big black oven until now we are all that is left of a great and magical circus . . .

GRETEL (*rounding on them*). You're not sorry for me or my
brother! You're only sorry for yourselves! (*To* MOFF *and*
SHOES.) When we met you we liked you so much we
wanted to be like you! How stupid we were! (*To* RAB.)
And you! You made me a promise! You said . . . You said
to me – 'I'll never let you fall.' (*Throws pipes to the ground
at his feet.*)

RAB. I've told you, we did what we had to do!

MOFF. You would have done the same! (GRETEL *looks at her
proudly.*) And don't think you wouldn't have! *(But she looks
away from* GRETEL*'s fierce gaze.)*

RAB. What's done's done! It's the way things are and you'll
just have to get used to it like everyone else.

GRETEL (*with contempt*). 'I'll never let you fall.'

RAB. If you're so clever, you fight the witch! Go on, let's see
you . . . You saw what happened to my father . . . Leave her,
she's not worth it.

MOFF. We've learned to look after ourselves, you should learn
to do the same! (*Goes with* RAB *into the maze of patchwork
tents.*)

SHOES. Fear has made us weak . . . So weak . . .

LOB. I know you can never forgive us, but we're sorry all the
same . . . We're sorry . . . (*Goes with* UNCLE SHOES *into
the tents.*)

GRETEL. Hansel . . . Please let him be alright . . . (S*he
uncovers the trailer.* HANSEL *lies back against the bars,
the tray beside him is empty.*) Hansel?

HANSEL. I've eaten all of it, Gretel . . . All of it . . . And if
there was more I'd eat it too . . .

GRETEL. The witch made you do it.

HANSEL. I'm so full I can't move . . . And now she'll cook
me and eat me for breakfast . . .

GRETEL. I won't let her!

HANSEL. How can you stop her? (*She has no answer.*) No sister, she's so strong she can do what she wants . . . You must run away from here.

GRETEL. Never!

HANSEL. Go on, run while you can! Go away and never come back!

GRETEL. Stop it! I'm your sister and I'll never leave you. (*Takes his hand.*)

HANSEL. I'm so glad of you . . .

Enter ORIN, *as silently as a dream.*

ORIN. How brave you both are!

GRETEL. The Faerie-King!

ORIN. Quiet, or she'll hear you!

HANSEL. Have you come to help us?

ORIN. She took my son, and she took The Staff Of The World's Magic . . . I have no magic to help you.

GRETEL. But how else can we fight the witch?

ORIN. The courage and love that lies inside your heart – it is the strongest magic of all. Trust me.

HANSEL. Why should we?

GRETEL. We trusted the circus people and they led us to the witch.

ORIN. Only because they have forgotten their courage and love . . . And remember, it wasn't just the circus people that led you here . . .

GRETEL. That's true . . . We followed our little white bird and it wouldn't betray us, it wouldn't lead us into harm . . . Oh, if only that were true!

STREGAMAMA (*from inside the caravan*). Keep the noise down out there!

HANSEL. The witch!

ORIN. Remember, you have magic of your own. Trust me, and do not be afraid . . .

GRETEL. I trust you . . .

ORIN vanishes as the caravan window slams open.

STREGAMAMA. Yak, yak, yak – how am I supposed to get to sleep? (*Sniffs.*) There's a smell of magic out here . . . Must be imagining it . . . Noisy little brats, if you must talk, talk quietly! Do I make myself understood?

GRETEL. Y-yes.

STREGAMAMA. Then goodnight! (*Slams the window shut.*)

GRETEL. Sssh, we must keep quiet . . .

HANSEL. He's gone.

GRETEL. Was he ever here, or did we just dream him? . . . But it is true about our bird.

HANSEL. What use is a bird? We're alone and there's no-one to help us . . . No-one in the world . . .

Enter MONKEY, *from the forest.*

GRETEL. Who's there? (MONKEY *retreats, prepares to run back into the forest.*) No, wait . . . (*Recognises him.*) Monkey! I'd forgotten all about you . . .

HANSEL. Ssssh! The witch!

GRETEL (*in a half-whisper*). You tried to warn us, I know that now . . .

HANSEL. But we didn't listen . . . (MONKEY *turns away from them, goes to a corner where he eats from a bowl on the ground like an animal, laps water from a rainbarrel.*)

GRETEL (*gently*). No, not like that . . . You're not an animal, are you? You're not really a monkey . . . (*He grunts and drinks.*) Here, like this . . . (*She dips her hands into the barrel, and offers him water from her cupped hands.*) I won't hurt you . . . (*He drinks from her hands.*) Thank you for trying to help us . . .

HANSEL. If only we had listened . . . (MONKEY *climbs onto the cage, looks in closely at* HANSEL.) I've stuffed myself with food . . . In the morning she will cook me . . . (MONKEY *grunts sadly.*) It's not your fault . . . (MONKEY *picks up a small, thin stick, pokes it through the bars to* HANSEL.) What are you doing? That's what the witch does . . . Stop it!

GRETEL. No, he's not poking you . . . He wants you to take it . . . (MONKEY *nods,* HANSEL *takes the stick.*)

HANSEL. But why? I don't understand.

MONKEY*, in imitation of the witch, swaggers imperiously up to the cage.*

GRETEL. He's pretending to be the witch. (MONKEY *feels the stick, grunts and stamps his foot angrily.*)

HANSEL. What's he doing?

GRETEL. I know!

STREGAMAMA (*from inside the caravan*). Quiet out there, or I'll boil you up for soup!

GRETEL (*in an excited whisper*). Listen, Hansel!   In the morning when the witch comes to see how plump you are, give her the stick to feel instead of your finger . . .

HANSEL. Then she'll think I'm still skinny . . .

GRETEL. And not worth eating . . . (*To* MONKEY.) That's right, isn't it? (MONKEY *nods.*) Clever Monkey!

HANSEL. It'll never work.

GRETEL. Yes it will! Remember, her eyes are weak . . . You are clever, Monkey!

HANSEL. I'm so tired, but I'll never sleep . . . I'm so cold and frightened . . . (MONKEY *goes into one of the tents.*)

GRETEL. Monkey?

HANSEL. He's gone . . . Everyone leaves us . . .

GRETEL. No, he's coming back . . . (MONKEY *comes back trailing two blankets, gives one to* GRETEL *and one to* HANSEL.) Thank you for the blanket . . . (*Wraps it around her shoulders.*)

HANSEL. But thank you most of all for coming back . . . (*Wraps himself up in blanket, lies down.*)

GRETEL. If only we could sleep then a dream might come and pull us up on a moonbeam and take us far away from here . . .

HANSEL. Far, far away . . . (MONKEY *picks up the pipes that* GRETEL *threw to the ground, and begins quietly to play a beautiful tune.*) What lovely music . . . Listen, it's saying – 'Don't be afraid, everything will be alright' . . .

GRETEL. Yes . . . And can you feel the moonbeam, Hansel, pulling us up and up, into the wind and out again?

HANSEL. I can feel it . . . I'm not frightened anymore . . . I'm not afraid . . . (*Sleeps.*)

GRETEL. Thank you, Monkey, you're a true friend . . . A true friend . . . (*Sleeps.*)

MONKEY *plays on until he notices that they are asleep, and then he puts down his pipes, lies down beside* GRETEL *and joins her in sleep.*

Scene Two

HANSEL, GRETEL *and* MONKEY *sleep on peacefully as birdsong commences and dawn breaks over the encampment.*

LOB *and* UNCLE SHOES *come wearily out from the tents.*

LOB. Rab, Moff, get up! Move yourselves.

SHOES. Soon the witch will wake, and we must serve her. (*Fetches chair and bucket.*)

Enter RAB *and* MOFF, *yawning and stretching.*

RAB. It can't be morning already . . .

LOB. It's morning . . . Hurry, or you'll be late.

> SHOES *stands looking down at* HANSEL, GRETEL *and* MONKEY, *who are still fast asleep.*

SHOES. See, brother, see how the innocent can sleep.

LOB. Let them lie . . . You're free when you sleep . . .

MOFF. Will they hate us forever?

RAB. Wouldn't you?

MOFF. Yes, for ever and ever . . .

> *A low, guttural moan comes from inside the caravan.*

SHOES. She wakes!

LOB. Quickly, we must be ready! (*They rush to gather brushes, cloths, bottles, a basin of water. The door of the caravan swings slowly open.*) She comes, she comes! (*After some confusion, they form into line, standing to attention like servants in the hall of a great house.*)

> LA STREGAMAMA *comes out of the caravan, bald and bare-footed.*

STREGAMAMA. I hate the mornings, and what a night I've had! My poor tummy . . . Leo The Lion's been fighting back, and my head's on fire . . . (*Sits in chair.*) Tossing and turning, some horribly uplifting tune going round and round in my poor head . . . (LOB *wets a cloth and places it carefully over her bald head.*) That's better, much better . . . (*To* MOFF.) Don't just stand there, girl – My hair, fetch my hair! (MOFF *rushes into the caravan.*) The sun hurts my eyes . . . I'm going to be sick . . . (*To* SHOES.) My bucket, fetch my bucket! (SHOES *rushes to obey.* MOFF *comes out of the caravan carrying the witch's red wig.*) Ah, my shining hair . . . I feel better already. (*Waves the bucket aside.*) Me boots! Where's me boots! (RAB *rushes into the caravan.*) I am going to be sick! (*Clutches her stomach.*) No, I'm not . . . Yes, I am . . . No, I'm not . . . Yes, I am! (*She is hugely sick into bucket held by* SHOES *until a lion's tail hangs over the bucket's side, and as she slowly lifts her*

head SHOES *must suffer her foul breath full in his face.*)
Hair now! Hair and boots! (MOFF *helps her on with her
wig,* RAB *helps her on with her boots.*) Get on with it!
Oh, I'm not at my best in the mornings . . . But now I'm
my beautiful self again I'll have a drink from my big bottle.
(LOB *hands her the big bottle, and she takes a real snifter
which makes her shake her head, and stamp her foot.*)
That's more like it! Now I'm ready for my breakfast! (*Claps
and rubs her hands in anticipation, turns to cage.*) But
they're asleep the little darlings, and my monkey-pet beside
them . . . . Awww, isn't it sweet how they can sleep when
I haven't had a good night's sleep for a thousand years?
(*Suddenly loud and fierce.*) Wakey-wakey! (HANSEL,
GRETEL *and* MONKEY *spring to their feet, dazed with
sleepiness and alarm.*) Inspection time! I must see how
plump he is . . . (*Pushes past* MONKEY *and* GRETEL.)
Out of my way . . . Inspection time! (*To* HANSEL, *poking
at him through the bars.*) Let me feel you, boy. Give me
your finger!

HANSEL (*still dazed*). My finger?

GRETEL. Your finger, Hansel . . . You know! (MONKEY
grunts and points.)

STREGAMAMA. Of course he knows! Keep your mouths
shut, the pair of you! (*To* HANSEL.) Your finger – this
minute!

HANSEL (*remembering, picks up stick*). My finger . . . Here
you are . . . (*Holds stick out to the witch.*)

STREGAMAMA (*in greedy anticipation*). How fine and
plump he will be, the lamb . . . (*Feels stick-finger.*) What's
this? (*Wails.*) Still skinny! Still skinny! (GRETEL *embraces*
MONKEY.) I don't want a skinny breakfast! (*Stamps
angrily.*) I want a big fat breakfast!

LOB (*impressed by the trick*). He's just a useless scrap . . .

SHOES. He's not worth the eating . . .

STREGAMAMA. But I had my heart set on him . . . My
whole heart! (*Paces, mutters.*) Unjust . . . Preposterous . . .
Unprecedented . . . (*Screeches.*) What's to be done?

RAB. You could leave him for a few weeks . . .

STREGAMAMA (*appalled*). Weeks?

MOFF. Or months.

STREGAMAMA. Impossible! I must think, think . . . It's coming to me, it's coming . . . Yes, that's it!

RAB. What's it?

STREGAMAMA. I'm going to eat him anyway.

GRETEL. But you can't!

STREGAMAMA. Why not, girlie? I want him and I always get what I want.

LOB. Think how much more there will be if you could only control yourself . . .

STREGAMAMA. I didn't get where I am by controlling myself! No, my mind's made up . . . I must light my roasting oven . . .

GRETEL. No, please, I beg you . . .

STREGAMAMA. You can beg all you like . . . (*Busies herself at oven.*)

GRETEL. He's my brother . . . I'll do anything . . .

STREGAMAMA. What can you possibly do for me?

GRETEL. Please!

STREGAMAMA. There's nothing you can do to save him. Absolutely nothing . . . Unless . . .

GRETEL. Unless what? Tell me!

STREGAMAMA. Unless you go into the forest and bring me back someone I can eat in his place . . . (*The circus people share a look of pity and horror.*)

GRETEL. Never!

STREGAMAMA. Suit yourself, girlie.

LOB. Then she would be like us.

STREGAMAMA. You're alive, aren't you? (*To* GRETEL.) I'll set him free, you have my promise . . . Of course, if you don't want to save your brother . . .

GRETEL. I didn't say that!

HANSEL. Don't listen to her!

STREGAMAMA. After all, stocks are getting low . . . If I'm not careful I'll have no-one left to eat . . . Go on, girlie.

HANSEL. No, Gretel!

STREGAMAMA. Save him!

GRETEL. I can't think . . .

STREGAMAMA. Bring me someone I can eat in his place . . . Go on . . .

HANSEL. No!

STREGAMAMA. It's the only way.

GRETEL (*in despair*). I'll go mad, mad! (*She runs off into the forest.*)

STREGAMAMA. That's my girl . . . (MONKEY *runs off after* GRETEL.) Go on, little Monkey, keep her company . . . (*To circus people.*) Go after her – Help her catch someone for me . . . Go! (*They go to follow* GRETEL, *but* LA STREGAMAMA *stops* MOFF *with her long stick.*) But you can stay here with me . . . (*To* LOB, RAB *and* SHOES.) Just in case you have any plans to run away . . . Go! (LOB, RAB *and* SHOES *run after* GRETEL.) Little Gretel was so good and brave, but soon she will be a coward like little Moff here. (*Opens cage, throws* MOFF *inside, slams door and locks it.*) A useless little coward!

HANSEL. My sister will never be like her!

STREGAMAMA. We'll see, dearie . . . We'll see . . .

MOFF (*kicking the bars like a wild animal*). Let me out of here! Let me out!

STREGAMAMA. Poor Moff . . . Did you think you were special, did you think you would never end up in my cage? (*Begins to laugh.*) Everyone ends up in my cage one day . . . Everyone . . . Everyone . . . (*Laughs and laughs and laughs.*)

Scene Three

The very heart of The Wild Forest. Enter GRETEL, *at a run.*

GRETEL. I've run and run, but I have nowhere to run to . . . Can't go on, can't go back . . . I'll never escape from this forest, and I'll never save my brother from the witch . . . Never . . .

Enter ORIN.

ORIN. Let your heart be brave.

GRETEL. You! I've tried to be brave, but everything just gets harder! How can you help me?

ORIN. You must help yourself, little girl . . . Or did you think I would do it all for you? No, the defeat of evil is never easy, and must be fought for with all your strength . . .

GRETEL. The Faerie-King – you're just a poor and weak old man . . . Leave me alone!

A noise from the trees.

ORIN. Who's there? (*Enter* MONKEY, *unseen by him.*) My son! Can it be true . . .

GRETEL. Monkey . . . (*Runs to embrace him.*)

ORIN (*seeing* MONKEY). I thought I had found him . . . But my son is lost to me . . . Lost . . . (*Staggers, almost falls.* MONKEY *and* GRETEL *go to his aid.*) Get him away from me! He is a witch's creature!

GRETEL. No, he is gentle and kind, and my only friend. (MONKEY *kneels to* ORIN.)

ORIN. It's true, he is kind to this poor and weak old man . . .
Forgive me, gentle creature . . .

RAB, SHOES *and* MOFF *can be heard in the distance calling out for* GRETEL.

GRETEL. They're looking for me!

ORIN. Then listen, for the truth is rare and must be respected!
Each one of us has a light that burns inside, a light of
courage and love, and every time we turn away from that
light, it grows dimmer and dimmer until we cannot see our
way in the darkness . . . If you ran away and left your
brother . . .

GRETEL. I would live forever in darkness.

ORIN. You know this in your heart.

GRETEL. There is another way.

ORIN. What other way?

GRETEL. I am too ashamed to say it.

ORIN. Say it.

GRETEL. The witch has promised . . . If I bring another to her,
she will free my brother . . .

ORIN (*an angry challenge*). Then take me, if you wish . . .
Come on . . . (*Makes to go.*) What are you waiting for?
Take me!

GRETEL. No.

ORIN. Why not?

GRETEL. It's what she wants . . . Nothing would put my light
out sooner . . . (*The calling voices grow louder.*)

ORIN. Blind her, blind her with your light! (*To* MONKEY.)
And you must help her . . .

GRETEL. I'm so afraid of La Stregamama . . .

ORIN. That is only a game she plays to amuse herself . . . Her
real name is Banshee, great high witch and mother of all

mischief. Remember this, for knowing her name gives you power . . . Kill her, and you kill all the witches in the world!

GRETEL. But she is so strong . . .

ORIN. It's your fear that makes her strong . . . Put away fear, little girl, put away fear and blind her with your light . . . (*He vanishes as* RAB, UNCLE SHOES *and* LOB *enter at a run.*)

RAB. We've found you!

LOB. Listen, Gretel!

SHOES. We have an idea!

LOB. Run as far and as fast as you can . . .

SHOES. We'll tell the witch you've been eaten by wolves.

GRETEL. I'd rather wolves than her ugly mouth.

RAB. Then go quickly! You can't save Hansel. Save yourself!

GRETEL. Tell me, Rab, where is your sister?

RAB. The witch has kept her.

GRETEL. Would you run away and leave her?

RAB. If there was no other way . . .

GRETEL. Would you?

RAB. No . . . Never.

GRETEL. Then why ask me to do it? I won't leave my brother.

RAB. We must help you find another to take to the witch.

GRETEL. No! If I did that I would be alive but my life would be over . . . I would be dead inside . . .

RAB. She thinks she's better than us!

SHOES (*to* RAB). It's the truth, you know it is.

LOB. But what will you do?

GRETEL. I'm going back to fight the witch.

RAB. What with? She'll cook you up and eat you.

GRETEL. Perhaps she will, but I won't be afraid any more . . .

SHOES. Good luck, little girl.

GRETEL. Monkey? (*He takes her hand.*) You make me strong.
(*Goes with* MONKEY.)

RAB. She's mad!

LOB. I am a hundred times stronger, but she . . . She is a
thousand times braver.

SHOES. If only we could be like her . . . Like we once were . . .
Come boy, come brother, let us help her if we can . . .
(*Exeunt in pursuit of* GRETEL *and* MONKEY.)

Scene Four

The circus encampment. MOFF *and* HANSEL *in the cage.*
MOFF *weeps quietly.*

HANSEL. Are you frightened? Are you lonely? So what! Now
you know what it's like . . . And stop crying!

MOFF. I'm not crying . . . I never cry! (*Cries.*)

HANSEL (*mockingly*). Oh no, of course not . . . (*Relents.*)
I never cry either, except when I'm crying . . .

MOFF. I've told you – I'm not crying!

HANSEL. If . . . If you were crying . . . Well, what good are
tears? They just make your face wet.

MOFF (*after an involuntary laugh*). You're right, and you're
kind, for one who should hate me . . .

Enter LA STREGAMAMA *with some logs for her oven.*

STREGAMAMA (*to her oven*). My dearest darling oven,
I have some logs for you . . . The sweetest logs . . . (*Sings to
herself.*)

I feed you, and you feed me,
How happy, warm and fed are we.

Soon you'll be roaring away as hot as The Cave Of Fires . . .
(*Rubs her head as if in pain.*) No, not that . . . Not The Cave
Of Fires . . . Well, boy, no sign of sister . . . (*Tuts.*) Are you
ready for the flames?

HANSEL. Vile witch! You don't frighten me.

STREGAMAMA. Oh but I do, I know I do, which is how I
like it, for fear adds such flavour to a dish . . . (*Fiercely.*)
Give me your finger again. Your finger! (MOFF *passes him
the stickfinger, and he holds it out to the witch who sniffs it
and pulls it from his grasp.*) A trick, a trick! You'll pay for
that! No-one tricks La Stregamama . . . (*Snaps sticks into
many pieces.*) I'll crunch your bones! (HANSEL *turns his
back on her.*) Don't you turn your back on me, you insolent
little brat! (*Unlocks cage eagerly.*) Out, out now! This
minute! I can't wait a moment longer . . .

MOFF. Leave him alone!

STREGAMAMA (*pushes* MOFF *roughly aside*). Let me at
him! (*Grabs* HANSEL *by the scruff of the neck.*) There'll be
no tricks this time! It's the oven for you, my boy! (*Drags
him purposefully out of cage.*)

Enter GRETEL *and* MONKEY *followed by the curious
circus people.*

GRETEL. No, witch – leave him be!

STREGAMAMA (*confused for a moment*). What? Who? . . .
(*Sees* GRETEL.) So you've come back, girlie. (*Grandly.*)
Well?

GRETEL. 'Well' to you too!

STREGAMAMA (*menacingly*). Don't play silly games . . .
Who have you brought for me?

GRETEL. No-one.

STREGAMAMA (*stunned*). No-one?

GRETEL. No-one.

STREGAMAMA. Impossible! She can't be this brave or this stupid.

HANSEL. My brave sister . . . (*Takes her hand.*)

GRETEL. My brave brother . . . If we must die, we must die together . . .

HANSEL. Together.

GRETEL. Only do not be afraid.

HANSEL. With you at my side – never . . . (MONKEY *joins them.*) And you, Monkey.

STREGAMAMA (*dizzy*). Outrageous! Never seen such courage . . . Makes my head hurt . . . (*Rears up.*) But, brave or not, it makes no difference to me! I'll cook you both! Watch me now! (*Casts spell –)*

Come burn and flame, and never tire,
Come burst with life, my roasting fire!

She aims a bolt of fire at her oven which bursts into roaring flames with such a terrifying urgency that everyone backs away from it.

You first, boy!

HANSEL. It's so hot, sister.

STREGAMAMA. And it shall be even hotter! More logs, and you girl, you will place them in my oven!

GRETEL. Do it yourself! (*Behind the witch's back,* MONKEY *mimes pushing her.*)

STREGAMAMA. Do what you're told!

GRETEL. But I don't know how.

STREGAMAMA. It's easy . . . Just open the door and throw them in.

GRETEL (*at the oven*). I can't get the door open . . .

STREGAMAMA (*with monumental impatience*). Oh get out of my way, and I'll show you! (*Mutters, opens door to oven.*) There! Nothing could be easier . . .

GRETEL *gives the witch a push and* LA STREGAMAMA *stumbles forward with flailing arms, struggling to keep from pitching headfirst into the hungry flames. All lean forward in excited anticipation.*

LOB. Burn, witch, burn!

ALL. Burn, witch, burn! (*But* LA STREGAMAMA *regains her balance and rounds on her enemies with savage fury.*)

STREGAMAMA. You'll never get me with that old trick!

HANSEL (*to circus people*). Come, stand with us.

GRETEL (*as* MONKEY *beseeches them silently*). Please . . . You're brave, I know you are . . . Stand with us! (*But they hang their heads and look away.*)

STREGAMAMA. They'll never stand against La Stregamama . . . They've lost their courage long ago, and they know La Stregamama is the strongest of all! (*Prods* HANSEL *towards oven with her long stick.*)

HANSEL. You're only strong when we're scared!

GRETEL. And that's not your real name!

STREGAMAMA. What did you say?

GRETEL. La Stregamama is only a game you play . . . I know your real name.

STREGAMAMA. No-one knows my real name . . . It is a witch's deepest and darkest secret.

GRETEL. I know your name, and I am not afraid.

STREGAMAMA. Tell me it, then . . . Come on, you stupid little brat, stop your boasting and tell me . . .

GRETEL (*with an instinctive power and formality*). I know you – you are Banshee, great high witch and mother of all mischief!

BANSHEE (*reeling, clutching at her head*). My name! She knows my secret name!

HANSEL. She grows weak . . . (*To circus people.*) Stand with us.

BANSHEE (*warningly*). Don't even think it! (*Clutches head, screeches.*) My head! My poor head!

GRETEL. Why be afraid of her when she is so ashamed of what she is she must hide behind another name?

HANSEL. Stand with us!

GRETEL. It is she who is the coward!

BANSHEE (*reaching down into her vast reserves of hatred and spite*). Back fools, and down! (*Casts a sway with her long stick.*) Down before me! (*All her enemies are sent crashing to the ground.*) You're dangerous, little girl . . . Very dangerous . . . (*Grabs GRETEL by her hair.*) The sooner you're in my oven the better! (*Drags her by the hair towards the oven.*)

HANSEL. My sister!

BANSHEE. Oh, I'm going to enjoy this! (*Prepares to fling her into oven.*)

SHOES. Wait!

BANSHEE. How dare you tell me what to do!

SHOES. There are others who would burn in her place.

BANSHEE (*witheringly*). And who might they be, clown?

RAB. I will burn in her place.

BANSHEE. What!!

MOFF. So will I.

BANSHEE (*staggers, lets go of GRETEL*). No! It can't be!

LOB. And I.

SHOES. And I, witch.

HANSEL (*taking MONKEY by the hand*). And us too.

BANSHEE (*in torment*). It can't be true! You're scared of me . . . Terrified . . . You're cowards . . . Cowards!

LOB. These children have shown us the way.

MOFF. We're not scared!

RAB. We're your slaves no more!

> BANSHEE *makes a bolt for it, but* UNCLE SHOES *stops her by placing one of his huge shoes against her and propelling her back towards the oven.*

HANSEL. Quickly, form a circle! Don't let her escape!

BANSHEE. You'll never beat me!

> *They encircle her, force her towards the oven.*

GRETEL. We're not scared, we're not scared . . .

> *The others take up the chant.*

ALL. We're not scared, we're not scared . . .

BANSHEE (*rallies terrifyingly*). Well you should be, you insolent worms! I am the cruellest of all! (*Casts a magical sway and scatters her enemy.*)

MOFF. She's too strong!

RAB. There's not enough of us!

BANSHEE. How right you are! You're no match for me! I'll cook you all, I'll cook you all!

GRETEL (*to* AUDIENCE). Please help us . . . Shout with us – 'We're not scared . . . '

BANSHEE. No!

AUDIENCE. We're not scared, we're not scared . . .

> HANSEL, GRETEL *and the circus people reform their circle and surround the witch.*

BANSHEE (*to* AUDIENCE). Be silent, brats! Be silent!

AUDIENCE. We're not scared, we're not scared . . .

BANSHEE. I'll roast you all! I'll roast you all . . . (*Rushes at* AUDIENCE, *but the circle holds firm and advances, forcing her nearer and nearer to her fate.*)

AUDIENCE. We're not scared, we're not scared . . .

BANSHEE *holds her long stick up threateningly, but* MONKEY *darts forward and snatches it from her.*

BANSHEE. Noooo!

AUDIENCE. We're not scared, we're not scared . . .

BANSHEE. Banshee hates you! She hates you all! (*Falls, screaming her hatred, into the roaring oven.* GRETEL *slams shut the oven door.*)

ALL shout and jump for joy. HANSEL, GRETEL *and* MONKEY *embrace.* LOB *embraces his children.*

SHOES. Thank you, Hansel and thank you, Gretel – you have saved us all.

HANSEL (*indicates* AUDIENCE). We had help from everyone.

The oven begins to hiss and steam and shake.

GRETEL. What's happening?

RAB. Look out!

LOB. It's going to blow!

MOFF. Everyone, get down!

They all throw themselves to the ground as the oven blows to bits in a mighty explosion. Enter ORIN, *strong again.*

ORIN. This wild forest, and all who live in it, give thanks, for your courage has conquered fear and delivered us from a great evil. (*Bows to* HANSEL *and* GRETEL.)

LOB (*amazed*). Who . . . Who are you?

GRETEL. The Faerie-King . . .

MONKEY. My father . . .

HANSEL. Your father?

MONKEY *turns to face them, and he is no longer a monkey-boy.*

ORIN. Conal, my son . . .

CONAL. The witch's magic kept me as her monkey-pet, but now I am free again.

ORIN. Forgive me, for I did not know you . . .

CONAL. No, father, it is I who must be forgiven . . . (*Kneels to his father.*) I let her take your staff of power and use it as her ugly stick . . . (*Bows his head and holds out staff.*) Take back your power – The Staff Of The World's Magic. (ORIN *takes the staff.*) Never let me hold it again . . .

ORIN. You are my true and only power . . . Get up onto your feet . . . In time I will gladly give this staff into your keeping, and the forest will know a great and true King of Magic . . . (*Embraces his son.*) All good magic is strong again . . . And now these children must be rewarded for their courage . . . (*Goes to caravan, strikes it with his staff and a secret compartment opens and disgorges three sacks of treasure.*) Come, Hansel and Gretel . . . It is all for you.

HANSEL. What is it?

ORIN. The witch's treasure . . . Open and see for yourselves.

HANSEL (*opening sack*). Gold . . .

GRETEL. And silver . . .

HANSEL. And precious stones . . .

GRETEL. It's lovely . . . But must we have it all?

ORIN (*laughing*). It is yours to do with as you wish.

GRETEL (*with a quick look to her brother*). Yes, Hansel?

HANSEL. Yes, sister.

GRETEL (*to* LOB). My brother and I would like you to have the largest sack.

LOB. No . . . It is yours to keep . . .

HANSEL. Please . . . (*Offers him the largest sack.*) Build again your magic circus . . .

GRETEL. And take it to all the great and far countries of the world . . .

HANSEL. Please take it . . .

LOB (*takes treasure sack*). How can we thank you?

RAB. We'll do what they wish . . . We'll build the greatest circus ever seen!

MOFF. We'll take the world by storm!

SHOES. And bring joy and mischief with us wherever we go!

ORIN. Then go on your way . . .

LOB *slings the sack over his shoulder.* UNCLE SHOES *puts on his drum, picks up his horn.*

RAB (*to* GRETEL). Once you said you wanted to be like us . . . Now we will try always to be as good and brave as you, who have given us back our courage and set us free . . . (*Kisses her hand.*)

MOFF (*to* HANSEL). Thank you for your kindness . . . I will give you a kiss . . . (*Kisses him.*) And one day, when we meet again, you may give me a kiss in return . . . Goodbye, sweet Hansel . . .

SHOES. And so you were lost, but look how you have found yourselves . . . Well done to both of you . . . Well done indeed . . . And so now it is time to make our farewells . . . It is a time that must be marked with great dignity and no little sadness . . . (*His trousers fall down.*) Every time the same . . . It can't be helped . . .

MOFF.
If I were a Queen
What would I do?
I'd make you King
And I'd wait for you.

RAB.
If I were a King
What would I do?
I'd make you Queen
For I'd marry you.

LOB. Come, my children . . . Come, brother . . . Goodbye, Hansel . . . Goodbye, Gretel . . .

HANSEL *and* GRETEL (*in unison*). Goodbye, goodbye . . .

> RAB, MOFF, LOB *and* UNCLE SHOES *go on their way, with* UNCLE SHOES *blowing his horn and beating his drum.*

ORIN. Time, children . . . Time to go home . . .

GRETEL. Oh yes, home . . .

HANSEL. But how will we find our way?

ORIN. Close your eyes, and think of home . . . Our magic will carry you home.

GRETEL. Magic?

CONAL. Hold my hands . . . That's it . . . Now close your eyes. (*They close their eyes,* ORIN *holds up his staff, and the forest begins to transform into their father's house.*) It's beginning . . . Can you feel it?

GRETEL. It's wonderful!

HANSEL. I feel like I'm diving to the bottom of the sea!

GRETEL. Or flying and flying as high as the stars!

CONAL. You are flying . . . You're flying on magic's back, into the wind and out again . . . Now open your eyes . . .

HANSEL. Father's house!

GRETEL (*urgently*). Where's father?

ORIN. He's here, have no fear . . . He's been looking for you . . . Looking and looking . . .

CONAL. We leave you to your father's care . . .

ORIN. But remember, when next you go into the wild forest, do not be afraid, for we will watch over you . . .

HANSEL. We won't be afraid.

GRETEL. You are true friends.

CONAL (*taking the pipes from around his neck*). I must give you these back . . .

GRETEL. Keep them, please . . . Play them sometimes, so we may hear . . .

CONAL (*with a bow*). As you wish . . . (GRETEL *kisses him on the cheek.*)

FATHER (*from off*). Who's there?

ORIN. Your father . . . Farewell, brave children . . . Your magic was the strongest and the best of all . . . (ORIN *and* CONAL *vanish.*)

Enter FATHER. *He does not see his children.*

FATHER. A hundred times I've heard their voices, and called out their names, but when I come running I find only light and air . . . I won't look again . . .

HANSEL. Father?

FATHER (*without looking*). That is Hansel.

GRETEL. Father?

FATHER. And that is Gretel . . . Time and time again I come running like a fool, but they're never here, they're never here . . . (HANSEL *and* GRETEL *come forward, and embrace their father.*) My children . . . My beloved children! You've come home! I must be dreaming . . . Let me look at you . . . Step back, and let me have a good look . . . (*He looks at them closely.*) But you've grown . . . Look how big and strong you are . . .

HANSEL. And look what we've brought, father! (*They open their sacks and pour treasure into their father's hands.*)

FATHER. More gold and silver than I have ever seen!

GRETEL. We'll never go hungry again.

FATHER. Wonderful children!

HANSEL. But where is our stepmother?

FATHER. I have sad news . . . Your stepmother is dead.

GRETEL. Dead?

FATHER. I banged my finger with my hammer and she laughed so much she fell down dead at my feet.

GRETEL. My poor father . . .

HANSEL. You must be lonely here without her.

FATHER. Now that you're home, I'll never be lonely . . . Never! But it's late and you must be hungry . . . Come and eat . . .

GRETEL. In the morning, father . . .

HANSEL. We're too tired to eat . . .

FATHER. Come on to bed, then, where it's warm . . . Come on . . . (*He leads them to bed.*)

HANSEL. I'm so tired, I can hardly stand . . . (*Falls onto bed.*)

GRETEL (*as she lies down*). Oh, at last . . . My own dear bed . . .

FATHER. It's so good to have you home again . . . I thought I'd lost you . . .

HANSEL (*sleepily*). You'll never lose us, father . . .

GRETEL (*sleepily*). No matter what, you'll never lose us . . .

FATHER. Welcome home . . . Sleep safe and warm in your bed tonight . . . Goodnight, Hansel. (*Kisses him.*) Goodnight, Gretel. (*Kisses her.*)

HANSEL *and* GRETEL (*in unison*). Goodnight, father. (*Their* FATHER *goes.*)

GRETEL. Hansel?

HANSEL. What?

GRETEL. Nothing . . . My brave brother . . .

HANSEL. My brave sister . . . Goodnight . . . (*A noise at the window, and they are both instantly awake.*)

GRETEL. Did you hear that?

HANSEL. I heard it!

GRETEL. There's something at the window!

HANSEL (*goes to the window, gives a cry of delight*). Oh, Gretel – look!

GRETEL. What is it?

HANSEL (*reaching out the window*). Come and see . . . (*He brings in something cupped in his hands, shows it to GRETEL.*)

GRETEL. Our little white bird! It's lovely . . .

HANSEL. It's as white as snow . . . And how brave . . .

GRETEL. The next time I follow you, little bird, you may lead me as far as you wish . . . (*Kisses bird.*)

HANSEL. You'll lead me into all the great and far countries of the world . . . (*Kisses bird, and lets it go out of the window.*) I can't wait . . . I can't wait . . . (*Lies back down.*)

GRETEL. It will all come soon enough . . . Go to sleep . . . (*Lies back down.* CONAL*'s pipes can be heard from the forest.*) Listen . . . He's playing his pipes . . . He was the poorest of creatures and all the time he was a prince . . . A prince of magic . . .

HANSEL (*dreamily*). What lovely music . . .

GRETEL (*dreamily*). Lovely . . . Can you feel the moonbeam, Hansel? . . . Pulling us up and up, into the wind and out again . . .

HANSEL. I can feel it . . . Sweet dreams, sister . . . (*Sleeps.*)

GRETEL. Sweet dreams, brother . . . Sweet dreams . . . (*Sleeps.*)

CONAL *continues to play his pipes.*

Curtain.

The Music

The following music by Savourna Stevenson has been used in previous productions of Hansel and Gretel. *Companies should also feel free to use their own music.*

DO YOU ASK WHAT THE BIRDS SAY?

Music by Savourna Stevenson, Christmas 1997

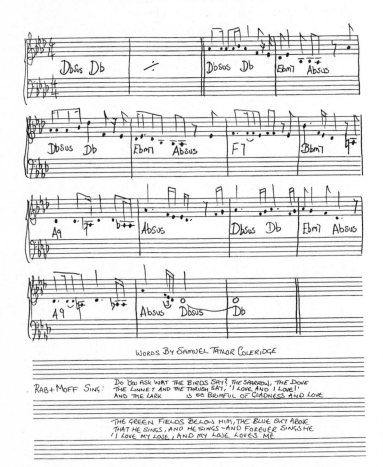

WORDS BY SAMUEL TAYLOR COLERIDGE

RAB + MOFF SING:

Do you ASK WAT THE BIRDS SAY? THE SAARROW, THE DOVE
THE LINNET AND THE THRUSH SAY, 'I LOVE AND I LOVE!'
AND THE LARK   IS SO BRIMFUL OF GLADNESS AND LOVE

THE GREEN FIELDS BELOW HIM, THE BLUE SKY ABOVE
THAT HE SINGS, AND HE SINGS — AND FOREVER SINGS HE
'I LOVE MY LOVE, AND MY LOVE LOVES ME

LA STREGAMAMA SINGS, *verses 1, 3, 5 and 6*

Music by Savourna Stevenson, Christmas 1997

Afterword

Children know more than adults – when they grow up they forget. Children know more because they think with their instinct not their reason. They carry the burden of what awaits them.
Krysztof Kieslowski

When I was four I was taken into hospital for an eye operation. But no-one had told me the full story. My parents, through misguided kindness, had not told me I would have to stay in, and hoped to steal away with as little fuss as possible. Suddenly they were waving at me through a window, and they were gone! My stomach lurched, fireworks exploded in front of my eyes, and there was a roaring sound in my ears. I was abandoned, alone! I barely managed to hold back the tears, and so began the whole ridiculous struggle to be brave. The seven-year-old girl who shared the ward with me seemed impossibly pretty and grown-up. And then there was the nurse! This severe and intolerant woman took an instant dislike to me. I imagined that my mother had insisted too forcibly that she be kind to me and thus had poisoned her irretrievably against me. The nurse took away my toys on the grounds that they were unhygienic. Together the seven-year-old girl and I stood against her and when she disappeared the next day we felt we had won a great and magical victory.

Years later, when a teacher read out the story of *Hansel and Gretel*, I felt dizzy, as if someone had spied on my dreams. This fairy-tale could not simply be a story. This, clearly, was the truth.

I think I understood then that good stories tell the truth about how difficult life can be, and therefore now when I write a play for children I try to satisfy their craving for seriousness every bit as much as their craving for fun and nonsense.

I have been lucky enough to see many excellent and bewilderingly different productions of my plays for children.

The best of them have been distinguished by directors, actors, designers and composers who can view seriousness and nonsense as more or less equal partners. (I may take fairy-tales seriously but there can be few pleasures as enjoyable as watching a dour Scottish actor climb inside a furry suit.) But there have also been some bad productions and the worst of these invariably mistake worthiness for seriousness, goodie-goodie cuteness for courage and knowingness for nonsense – a deadly, depressing mix.

A large family audience wants and deserves a more genuine and powerful form of dramatic story-telling than it usually gets from pantomime. And yet there is much to be learned from the music-hall bravado of panto, and I try to be true to what I understand as the magic of fairy tales without losing any of the energy, vulgarity and mischief of good panto. If there's an equation it's this – taking the story seriously, telling it clearly, and asking the audience to believe in it equals far more fun. An audience only really laughs when it cares about the story.

An attempt to achieve this balance in the theatre tends to correspond with the balance already present in fairy-tales. The 'Cinderella' story, for instance, tells us many important truths – that life is often cruelly hard, but if we hang on to our better instincts a happy future is possible; that the love of a parent for its child (presented in the shape of the graveside tree and the ancient hearth) does indeed have the power to transform the world; that the longed-for triumph of good over evil is far from automatic and must be striven for; that inner freedom affords the key to our courage and identity. And yet, while we may need the story for its ability to remind us of these, and many other truths, we love it for its romance, its mischief, and its magic. In writing my play *Cinderella* it was as important to have the dog pee in Puff's cake as it was to replace the familiar pumpkin-coach with the older and far more beautiful image of the graveside tree. To me this kind of robust vulgarity is true to the spirit of the tale, for *Cinderella*, like all fairy-tales, belongs to the folk. It often feels that these great stories have crawled out of the swamp with us, fulfilling what Tolkien described as 'the imaginative satisfaction of ancient desires' and it's as if we have all miraculously had a hand in the writing of them.

Sometimes I'm asked 'Do you only write for children' or 'Do you do any real writing?' Isaac Singer came up with a memorable reply to these questions:

> Children are the best readers of genuine literature. Grown-ups are hypnotised by big names, exaggerated quotes and high-pressure advertising . . . The child is still the independent reader who relies on nothing but his own taste . . . Names and authorities mean nothing to him . . . No matter how young they are, children are deeply concerned with so-called eternal questions. Who created the world? Who made the earth, the sky, people, animals. Children cannot imagine the beginning or the end of time and space . . . Children think about and ponder such matters as justice, the purpose of life, the why of suffering. They often find it difficult to make peace with the idea that animals are slaughtered so that man can eat them. They are bewildered and frightened by death. They cannot accept that the strong should rule the weak.

Isaac Bashevis Singer
Are Children the Ultimate Literary Critics?

This is true and inspiring, even when it sometimes seems that brand-names are more important to children than justice or the why of suffering. I wish I could have written such a wise and uncompromising statement of belief.

Stuart Paterson